The
Still Point

The
Still
Point

The Simplicity of
Spiritual Enlightenment

KEVIN KRENITSKY, MD

Waterside Productions
Cardiff-by-the-Sea, California

Printed in the United States of America

First Printing, 2022

ISBN-13: 978-1-954968-82-0 print edition
ISBN-13: 978-1-954968-83-7 ebook edition

Waterside Productions
2055 Oxford Ave
Cardiff, CA 92007
www.waterside.com

CONTENTS

INTRODUCTION

This book is about discovering and living as your indestructible, true self, which is deeper than just the body and the mind. Your true self could be called by any number of names, but we have chosen to call it the Still Point. To make the most of this book, it's important to glimpse the Still Point as a felt "experience" rather than just a mental concept. This is the experience of recognizing your own awareness, which is always with you. It is quite simply being aware of being aware. This is not some angelic or enlightened awareness you will obtain one day after much meditation, but the simple awareness with which you are aware of these words right here and right now. Right now, close your eyes and ask yourself, "Am I aware?" This is the very awareness with which you hear sounds, see sights, and know your thoughts. This is not about the "things" of which you are aware, but just the awareness that knows those things. When you ask yourself, "Am I aware?" you will recognize immediately that yes, you are aware. It's true that you will at first recognize this because of the sights, sounds, or thoughts of which you are aware, and that's fine. Ignore the many things you can be aware of and just relax into the experience of being aware itself. This glimpse of awareness is the Still Point, your true being. Once you have recognized this, you can return over and over again when you sit "formally" in meditation or even in the course of normal everyday activities. No matter what experience you are having, you can always ask, "What is it that knows this experience?" This too will take you to the awareness that is present and "knows" any experience you have.

This simple, natural feeling of being aware is your connection to the peace and happiness you are seeking. This is the Still Point, and it is unbroken peace itself. While the Still Point is peace and happiness, the reason you do not always feel peaceful and happy is that it has become "obscured," mainly by the thoughts and feelings that seem to cover it up. Spend as much time as needed in recognizing your self-aware being, because when you do, you can begin to remove the blocks to the happiness that is always available to you. That is the aim of this book.

Authors note:

Much of the book came to be written in a question-and-answer format. While several questions were asked by outside people, most were my very own questions, with some variations, asked by myself to myself over the years, prior to the writing of the book. Self-discovery is ultimately a solitary recognition, and in most cases, the mind must come to its own highest understanding before it successfully dissolves into its source. The Q&A format is intended to bring practical understanding in the form of answers to concepts that can seem foreign to minds still fixated on, and identified with, the transient.

PART
I

The
Still Point

"For nothing has ever

been said about God

that hasn't already been

said better by the wind

and the pines."

~ THOMAS MERTON

1

THE DISCOVERY OF OUR TRUE NATURE

*"No one can find you, so be no one
and find yourself."*

Our lives have both a dynamic quality and a static quality to them. Our experiences are dynamic, changing all the time. Our thoughts and feelings come and go like the summer wind. Sights and sounds also appear and disappear constantly. We taste food and enjoy the brief but satisfying aromas and flavors that disappear almost as quickly as they came. Even in dreams the states of experience change and morph rapidly. These are the dynamic aspects of our lives. Ever changing like the clouds passing in the deep blue sky. There is also the static quality of our lives. The deep unmoving backdrop of awareness in which all of the dynamic aspects of life come and go. This is the aspect that knows or makes all experience possible to be experienced. This is the Still Point. It is the ground of your very being. It is the ground of all being.

It is not only the ground of all being.
It is ALL BEING

3

It does not waver or come and go. Without its presence you could not see or hear anything. No thought or feeling would ever be possible. It's the seemingly hidden aspect of life that makes all experience possible. The Still Point has been called by many names throughout the ages. Awareness, Consciousness, Knowing, Being, Holy Spirit, Presence, Tao, and so forth, and the list goes on and on. It is what you have called "I" when referring to yourself your entire life. When you come to recognize the Still Point as what you actually are—the changeless aspect of you—a shift in identity begins to occur. A shift away from the belief that we are only the changing dynamic aspect of life such as our thoughts and feelings. In time this shift deepens, and life becomes more peaceful and carefree. Relationships improve and decisions and actions flow seamlessly from this deep place of infinite intelligence. All it takes to recognize the Still Point is to relax your attention from the constant focus on the dynamic aspect of life. After the recognition of the Still Point as your deepest reality, you come to see the dynamic aspects of life are nothing more than the Still Point in motion. There is a seamless freedom that emerges from this recognition. It is a freedom that comes not from intellectual understanding but rather from a knowing certainty. Life may outwardly look exactly the same after this shift in identity occurs, or it could change dramatically. Regardless, life is now lived from a completely fresh perspective. You have regained your freedom and dropped your resistance to all experience. When challenges arise, as they do for everyone, you approach them in a dramatically different way than before. You meet them exactly as they are without adding mental anguish or confusion to them. In this way, they resolve easily back into the Still Point that accepts everything without judgement. The freedom of true living is regained, never to be lost again.

4

"It is the Divine Presence that gives value to life. This presence is the source of all peace, all joy, all security. Find this presence in yourself and all your difficulties will disappear."

~ MIRA ALFASSA, "THE MOTHER"

The great secret of human existence is that you yourself are this deathless, unharmable Still Point of being. When you know, this living is a joy. The simple sense of awareness you feel as "I am" is the link you have in every moment to this astounding truth. We all know we are aware beings, but most of us fail to recognize that the awareness at our core is shared by all beings. It is one unified being; the Still Point from which we all experience life. The experience of having a body happens inside of this awareness, but we have been mistakenly conditioned to believe that we are only the body and thus will die when the body dies. This mistaken belief is the cause of all of our fear, anxiety, and worry. It is the cause of all the trouble we have in our relationships and the root cause of all the wars and strife in human history. You are here to discover what you really are and to live your life from this newfound realization of freedom and peace. If, as you are reading this, there is even the slightest sense that this is true—that you are something more than a limited creature with a short, often troubled lifespan—you have already begun to strip away the layers of conditioning that have kept you imprisoned. There is nothing in this world you could obtain or acquire that could even remotely compete with the power of this realization. The only thing you have to lose in coming to this realization of your true unlimited nature as the Still Point is the insane conditioning of the ego, which has brought you nothing but fear, worry, and conflict. As more and more people come to this realization, the very fabric of this planet's society is being radically changed for the better. The time has come for all of us to reclaim this understanding and finally live lives as full, complete human beings and not fearful clusters of deeply ingrained egoic conditioning. The golden era for all starts with the recognition of truth by one. There is no time to waste.

The mandated isolation imposed around the coronavirus outbreak gave many an opportunity to examine their lives in a way rarely seen before. Schedules, previously filled to the brim with constant movement, came to a screeching halt. During this time of relative isolation, the desire to procure lasting peace and stability regardless of outside circumstances blossomed. For many, these strange and unusual events served as a catalyst to begin a search to discover the changeless "place of peace" within. Others, already on the path of self-discovery for years or decades, found opportunity in the newfound isolation to deepen this practice.

This recognition of our true nature is often first experienced as a glimpse or a flash of peace or a moment of joy. At first, it's usually fleeting and quickly eclipsed by the return of our conditioned thoughts and emotions of fear, worry, or anxiety. But over time, as we revisit this Still Point of being, it becomes ever more stable, eventually remaining present in the midst of normal everyday experience. Our old conditioned patterns of thinking and acting start to soften, and in time fade into a completely new way of living. A way of life that is no longer in a constant fight to control our experience but rather lets our experience be exactly as it is. We begin to see the magical effects of not fighting the world and something extraordinary happens. The world stops fighting back. This doesn't mean experience changes at first necessarily, but it does mean the same experiences you had before are now much more enjoyable. This is the fruit of the labor that comes from finally giving emphasis to The Still Point. It means not being exclusively focused on our continually changing feelings or our constant chattering thoughts. This ultimately is what is meant by most of the great spiritual traditions that have implored us to build our homes on a solid rock-like foundation, the ever-present Still Point of being, and not on the continually shifting sands of our outside lives.

SELF DISCOVERY

The discovery of our true nature of being is more of a recognition of something that has been veiled in us rather than the discovery of something new. You are already yourself and you carry your sense of being with you everywhere. The one thing you always know, at least in the waking state, is this very sense of being or existence. The truth is this being knows itself through all states, including dreaming and deep sleep, but we will come around to that later. Because this being is your very own being it is always an act of pure self-recognition. No teacher can impart this reality to you. Anyone who has come to see this truth has done so alone. Teachers and books or words of any kind can only point to the truth but never take you there. The real discovery is self-discovery.

Although there are an unlimited number of seeming paths to this recognition, they all culminate with the simple but profound realization that what we essentially are is this unchanging awareness at the heart of all experience. The sensations of the body and the perceptions of the world all appear in our very own being. It's what is present and aware when a thought arises and that by which all thoughts are known. However, unlike thought, it is continuous and present between thoughts. It is what everyone refers to when they call themselves "I."

The only way we can collectively change the experience of our world for the better is by this recognition of our true nature of being. When any one person discovers their ever-present nature, they discover everyone's ever-present nature because we all share this one being. There are not billions of peoples living on this planet each with their own separate unique awareness but one unified awareness that is shared by all of us. This simple discovery that the core of our being is shared unites us all in that recognition. The awareness with which we all know whatever experience we are having at the time is this universal being. So, you see when we each wake up to our true nature, we realize it is everyone's true nature and we essentially free everyone from the illusion of separation that has been the cause of all our anger, animosity, and fear. This false belief in separation has been the cause of all our wars and strife throughout history. The greatest contribution to our society anyone can make is to recognize their own self, which is the same self of everyone. The real revolution is a revolution of one.

α: *How does one recognize this self you call the Still Point of being?*

Ω: Ask yourself the question, "Am I aware?" When you ask this of yourself, you go to the experience of being aware. After asking the question, there is a brief interval of no thought where the experience of being aware is obvious. It's worth mentioning that it's not an experience in the classic sense, but rather a knowing that you, awareness, are present.

α: *Yes, I am aware, but it can't be that simple, can it?*

Ω: It is that simple. In that instant after asking the question, you become aware of being aware. Awareness is aware of itself. Don't make the mistake of thinking this is a trivial discovery because being aware of being aware is the ground of happiness itself.

α: *It is obvious but seems too simple.*

Ω: And that is why it's overlooked by virtually everyone. It's not overlooked because it is some distant exotic revelation but rather it's so close and so intimate it's ignored in favor of the constant stream of thoughts and feelings we mistakenly take to be who we are. This is why anyone who goes on a spiritual search to find themselves ultimately ends exactly where they began at the simple sense of being we all call "I."

α: *So, the spiritual path is circular?*

Ω: In reality, there can't be a path to where you already are standing. This very conundrum is what the comparative mythologist Joseph Campbell referred to as the hero's journey. It's also reflected in the story of the prodigal son from the Bible. The son, initially safe at home in his father's kingdom, assumes there must be "more" out there. So, he leaves home and journeys to the far ends of the earth seeking something better. He becomes progressively disenchanted and lost, finally realizing he had everything at home. Thus begins the long journey to where he started. In fact, this is "a journey without distance to a place one never left," as described in *A Course in Miracles*.

α: *What is the practice to realize this then?*

Ω: Returning again and again to the Still Point of awareness, simply being aware of being aware. This is the essence of meditation. Simply resting as or being that awareness knowingly. In time, it's clearly seen that thoughts arise within this vast awareness and fade back into awareness. In fact, because thoughts are not aware, it's seen that not only do thoughts arise and fall in this awareness, but they are known by awareness and ultimately made out of awareness.

α: *Being aware seems obvious but you also talk about being. Are they the same?*

Ω: Awareness, our true nature, has many names in many traditions. Being, Consciousness, Knowing, Presence, Holy Spirit, and Tao are some examples of words that are synonymous with awareness. They can be used interchangeably.

α: *If this recognition is so important why is it not taught in our educational or religious systems?*

Ω: A significant majority of people in the world are still looking for happiness and fulfillment in outside experiences such as money, status, relationships, and altered states of mind seen with the use of recreational drugs. One must clearly see that lasting peace and happiness can never be found "out there." This need to "turn inward" is the core of most religious and spiritual teachings, but this teaching has been lost in the day-to-day application in favor of worshipping a deity or God that is "out there" in some remote place called Heaven or nirvana.

α: *What is the biggest obstacle to this awareness?*

Ω: Awareness, or being, is what you are eternally. If you feel happy in any given moment you are aware of feeling happy; if you are depressed you are aware of feeling depressed. Feelings come and go but the awareness that knows them is always present. You, awareness, are always present. You have simply not recognized this awareness as what you really are fundamentally. Many people still live life almost exclusively caught up in their thoughts and feelings, missing entirely the ever-present awareness without which no thought or feeling could ever be known. Examine this closely, contemplate this deeply. Return again and again to this awareness that is your very being until it's completely obvious that what you have called "I" all your life is eternally present awareness.

α: *I am not aware during sleep though?*

Ω: In the dream state, you are aware of the dream and all its aspects. During deep sleep, there is no experience to be aware of like in the waking or dream state, but awareness is aware of itself. This is why deep sleep is so peaceful and something we look forward to every night. If awareness disappeared during deep sleep we would not enjoy it but we do enjoy it tremendously. In fact, there is no "us" enjoying "it." Awareness, our self, enjoys itself by being aware of itself alone.

If you strip away everything that can be known, does knowing itself not remain? You are that knowing. Realize that and be free.

3

THE SEDUCTION
OF THOUGHT

When our true nature as the Still Point of aware-being is over-looked, we tend to live almost exclusively in our thoughts and feelings. Because of this exclusive attention to thoughts, we wrongly assume awareness, like thought, comes and goes. Because most of us are only focused on thinking, we mistakenly believe awareness is temporary and limited. We overlook its ever-present nature, as well as its unlimited nature. Because of this imagined loss of our unlimited nature, the fear of lack is born. Likewise, because of the belief in being tempo-rary, the fear of death arises. If you examine this closely you will find one of these two false beliefs at the core of every single fear you have.

Most people lead their entire lives driven by these fears. This is tragic because neither belief is true. The Still Point, our true nature, knows no lack and doesn't die. Imagine your quality of life if you had no belief in lack and felt whole and complete always. Add to that no fear of death or dissolution and life would be peaceful and happy. Not dependent on any external circumstance for peace and happiness at all. As the great Indian sage of the twentieth century Nisargadatta Maharaj said:

When the mind is kept away from its preoccupations it becomes quiet. If you do not disturb this quiet and stay in it, you find it is permeated with a light and a love you have never known; and yet you recognize it at once as your own nature. Once you have passed through this experience, you will never be the same person again; the unruly mind may break its peace and obliterate its vision; but it is bound to return, provided the effort is sustained; until the day when all bonds are broken, delusions and attachments end and life becomes extremely concentrated in the present.

α: *So, is this concentration in the present the same as living in the now?*

Ω: Yes. The Still Point, your true nature, is always experienced as here and now. It is timeless and changeless; in fact, it is outside of time and space. Any experience you or anyone has ever or could ever have was experienced in the now. When you had an experience of your fifth birthday party it was now in your experience. If you remember your fifth birthday party, it is a thought you are having now. It's inescapable. Try to step out of the now into the past or future. It's completely impossible.

α: *Why does the present now often not feel peaceful?*

Ω: It's because you are following thoughts into a regretful past or a worrisome future. This is the seductive power of thought and the single greatest cause of normal everyday tension or unrest. There is nothing normal about it, in fact.

α: *What is one to do about these unproductive thoughts?*

Ω: Nothing to do but only to be. Awareness or being is not a doing at all. Once this simple awareness is recognized, you return to it over and over again until thoughts are seen like clouds passing in the summer sky. Not to be followed or chased unless practically necessary in the moment.

α: *But when I am fearful or anxious, I can feel it not just as thought but as a sick-like feeling in the chest or stomach.*

Ω: Yes, most emotions have a seemingly physical component that when combined with accompanying thoughts creates the experience of fear or anxiety. In this case, it is most helpful not to avoid the experience, but to turn in and face it directly. If you close your eyes you will see this so-called physical component is experienced as a vibration in the field of awareness. Do not label it or add any thought to it at all. Isolate it without the addition of thought because that is where the worry can get out of hand and turn into panic. It's very important to welcome this sensation. Even if this is possible for only a short time at first, it is very helpful. Then if it becomes too much you can resort to other approaches, like going for a walk or a run in nature, until sitting with these sensations in complete acceptance becomes possible.

α: *So, is thought the enemy of this approach? Should one eliminate thought in meditation?*

Ω: No, a mind that is strictly controlled is not a free mind. Thoughts in themselves are not the problem but attaching oneself to thoughts as your identity is a problem. It's true that the vast majority of thoughts of one who has not yet recognized their true nature as awareness are unproductive or downright toxic, but they spring from the underlying faulty assumption of being a separate isolated self. Once it is clearly seen that our true nature is unified awareness, unproductive thoughts are simply dismissed.

When you are rooted in being and not thinking, when thoughts do occur, they reflect the character of being—peace and spaciousness, namely.

α: *Is recognition of the Still Point of awareness as oneself what is known as spiritual awakening or enlightenment?*

Ω: Spiritual awakening or enlightenment is the simple recognition of awareness as one's true irreducible nature and the further recognition of its innate or intrinsic properties. Namely that it can't be harmed or affected in any way and that it does not come or go. It is birthless and deathless and completely fulfilled.

α: *Is this a transcendent experience that happens at once?*

Ω: This recognition is transcendent of experience and not an experience at all. The recognition of self does not happen in time with thought but is literally outside time. It's possible that it can trigger a mild or profound relaxation of the body and mind, but this is variable and not the recognition itself. This often creates confusion that this relaxation is the realization, but it is at best a pleasant side effect.

α: *What is the experience of life like after such a recognition?*

Ω: Life gradually becomes more peaceful and happier. This is not an intellectual understanding but a felt knowing understanding. In fact, if it remains just an intellectual understanding it has no practical benefits, and what is the point? Instead of calling the understanding enlightenment or awakening it should be called peace and happiness, which is lived in every moment. Felt in every moment. That is what every single person actually wants.

α: *Before one can live a happy, peaceful life must not the ego be eliminated?*

Ω: The ego is the misidentification of yourself with form. Not just body form but thought forms in the shape of thoughts, images, and the feelings that accompany them. In this direct approach when we see clearly that we are the unchanging ever-present Still Point of awareness in which all these forms come and go, we recognize the unreality of the ego. It is true that the deep conditioned patterns of the ego then begin to recede, allowing one to live more in the now without the addition of self-limiting thoughts and beliefs added.

THE DIRECT
APPROACH

The approach to discover our true nature as the Still Point of unlimited awareness we are discussing here is very direct. We ask ourselves, "Are we aware?" or "What is it that knows my experience?" be it the thoughts that arise or the sights and sounds of the perceived "outside world." In that instant, we go visit the experience of being aware. We ideally see that we are not the thoughts, sights, sounds, smells, or textures we feel but that undefinable awareness in which all that experience arises. We do this over and over again in meditation, and also in the midst of our day-to-day experience, until this recognition of self as awareness becomes obvious.

Regardless of where one starts on the spiritual search, or simply the search for peace and happiness (because they are the same), one must have this glimpse or recognition of self. There are many progressive paths to self-realization that attempt to gradually prepare or cleanse one for this recognition of self as awareness. In fact, because progressive paths are so numerous—from various forms of mantra meditation to wonderful non-dual teachings like *A Course in Miracles*—there is a misunderstanding that this direct approach is new age or just new. This is not quite accurate, although it does seem to be gaining in popularity. Jesus himself taught the critical importance of "going within" to directly experience the self as pure awareness when in the Gospel of Matthew, he taught his disciples that "whenever you pray, go into a dark room alone and withdraw attention from the senses in order to come to a direct experience of God." This practice has been termed Hesychasm, from the Greek *hesychia*, meaning "stillness" or "silence." Although the seeming availability of very direct approaches to the recognition of the self as unlimited awareness was limited in the last few centuries, there were several Indian teachers of the twentieth century who resurrected this approach and helped bring it more into the mainstream. The well-known sages Ramana Maharshi, Atmananda Krishna Menon, and Nisargadatta Maharaj all taught very direct approaches to the recognition of our true and irreducible selves as this unlimited awareness that is our direct experience in every moment.

Nothing transient will ever satisfy you
No-thing at all will ever satisfy you
So, find that which is neither
transient nor a thing
This alone is satisfaction itself

α: *How does one know if a progressive or direct path to awakening or happiness is right for them?*

Ω: Whatever path one finds themselves on is the right path in that moment. If you are reading this and it rings true, then you are meant to take a direct approach, at least for now. Likewise, when people come across a progressive path and it deeply resonates with them then it is right for them at that time. The teaching finds the student and not the other way around. Years ago when *A Course in Miracles* fell into my lap, there was a near instant recognition of excitement that it was right at that time. Over a decade later, the direct path came to me in the very same way. This is more often than not the way it happens. When the student is ready the teacher will appear.

α: *Why would one not choose a more direct approach as opposed to a more roundabout way to happiness?*

Ω: Every seemingly separate mind is different in the way it is "contracted" and thus unique in terms of what teaching will help it the most to shed its conditioning and open to its true nature of eternal, infinite awareness. I remember in my early years of studying non-duality, David Hoffmeister, *A Course in Miracles*-based teacher, would employ a similar direct approach. People would come to him with a dizzying array of common everyday problems and he would always steer them back from the specifics of the ego "problem" they described to the one universal problem of believing they were separate isolated selves to the recognition they have never separated from the one mind we all share: the Still Point of universal awareness or being. At the time, it was not understandable to me but became very clear over time. He was simply using a more direct approach to the recognition of the one true problem and the one true solution, or recognition, within the context of the teachings of *A Course in Miracles*. You see regardless of the teaching and its progressive or direct nature, this direct recognition of our true being as awareness is necessary. It doesn't matter if the path one is on is called Zen Buddhism, Advaita Vedanta, Christian Mysticism, Taoism, *A Course in Miracles*, quantum physics, and the list goes on and on ad infinitum. At some point, one must recognize this glimpse of reality so the progressive establishment in this truth of our peaceful, unlimited being can directly affect our living experience.

α: *Don't some people have this recognition all at once and remain thereafter grounded in it or free of the ego mind thereafter?*

Ω: Yes, but it's extremely rare and has its own price to pay in terms of reintegrating the understanding into the body-mind and the experience of everyday life. Most have heard the story of Ramana Maharshi, who had the sudden recognition of his true nature at the age of sixteen, after just a very short time questioning the nature of reality. He spent years living in a cave as this understanding became integrated into how he lived, communicated, and used his body. There are other more recent examples of sudden realization or awakening as well. Eckhart Tolle comes to mind.

α: *The price to pay is slowly relearning how to function in the world then?*

Ω: Yes, one could say that, but after the sudden recognition of self, your happiness and peace is always apparent. So you see, regardless of living on a park bench or in a cave for a year or more you are happy. This is true regardless of what the outside circumstances are at the time. We are so deeply conditioned as humans to seek happiness in outside circumstances many keep looking for happiness and fulfillment there despite the fact that outside circumstances have never made anyone lastingly happy.

α: *But sudden explosive awakening or realization of self is not the way most have this recognition?*

Ω: No, it's extremely rare. Most people have an initial glimpse that they are the Still Point of awareness that knows all experience. There is certainly some freedom in this initial recognition alone. After this glimpse, many have some initial relaxation of the lifelong contraction of the body and the mind. For example, some people will experience less of the constant chatter of unproductive thoughts and find they not only think less but also experience more peace and much greater efficiency of mind. As they abide more and more as the awareness they recognize themselves to be, the very nature of awareness, our very being itself, reveals itself more and more. This is where we see a progressive weakening of our long-conditioned ego habits. This is the progressive relinquishment of fear and the realignment of our experience of life to more closely resemble the peace and happiness of our true nature of awareness.

α: *Why does something that sounds so easy in theory, namely the recognition of our self as awareness, seem so hard in practice?*

Ω: Humans have been almost exclusively obsessed with the content of our experience such as our thoughts, sights of the world, sounds, tastes, smells, and so on that we have over-looked that which allows them all to be known in the first place. Because awareness has no objective qualities at all, it's overlooked. It's the same when most people watch a movie. They see everything that changes such as the characters and the constantly changing scenes of the movie, but they over-look the absolute undivided nature of the screen. You, aware-ness, are the screen. Ever present, unchangeable and fully accepting of whatever happens in the movie, be it peaceful or violent.

α: *So, awareness is not something that can be known?*

Ω: Not in the way the mind knows objects. But remember there is nothing to the mind but thoughts and images and they arise from awareness and are known by awareness. The mind can't know awareness like it knows a thought, so while one can't know awareness, one can be awareness knowingly.

α: *Then being awareness knowingly is the path to freedom and happiness?*

Ω: Being or awareness is what you already always are, it's what all sentient beings already always are so it's not a path per se. You may call it a pathless path, but its more the rec-ognition that our true nature of awareness is already always present and self-aware. Thinking is nothing but a movement of awareness within awareness, but until awareness is recog-nized as always present, thinking seems to "take one away" or obscure its self-aware substratum. In reality, that is impossi-ble. So, at first, we ask ourselves, "Am I aware?" and with the recognition of awareness, we rest, as it were, there with and as ourselves. When resting as our true nature of awareness with our eyes closed, we allow thoughts and sensations to simply come and go. We see their transient rising from this eternal, limitless awareness that is both their source and destiny. Over time, this awareness seems to "brighten," and the power of thoughts and sensations to pull one away diminishes. As this recognition deepens, we stand as awareness in the midst of everyday activities. When thoughts and activities of everyday life no longer cause us to retract back into association with the thinking mind, we remain in presence and living becomes transformed over time. Life becomes more peaceful and your thoughts—and actions, when needed—become much more productive given whatever situations you are facing.

α: *When I rest in meditation as awareness, it seems to be a black space or field without limits, or at least no limits I can detect.*

Ω: Yes, that borderless "space-like" presence is as close as the mind can ever come to the completely nonobjective reality of the unlimited Still Point. The thinking mind can never find or make sense out of our true nature because it can only make sense out of things having objective, measurable qualities. This is not a problem as long as one doesn't try to objectify the space-like presence of awareness. Simply be that presence knowingly and in time it reveals its ever-present, unlimited nature in the way of a knowing understanding.

5

THE SPIRITUAL GPS

Every single person has an internal GPS that is constantly and gently trying to steer them to this understanding of their own true nature. Almost everyone has had the experience of something that was truly interesting or exciting to them that they passed on because of fear. Maybe they stayed in a job they disliked because of the fear of not having enough money to live. How many of us have dedicated years of our lives to higher education not because we loved what we were studying, but because we thought it would provide us security in the future? Not only are we not "following our bliss," as the comparative mythologist Joseph Campbell implored, but we are trudging ahead out of fear that is either subtle or extremely obvious. Doing what we love is immensely empowering and practical because, without perhaps knowing it, you are on the road to self-discovery. In addition, the output of work, or art, is very powerful when it comes from a place of love. Of course, it's true that for a time we may need to work in a suboptimal job for practical purposes, and in that time it's necessary to accept it and perform the job from this place of acceptance. As one returns over and over to their true nature of awareness and becomes more established in its peace, often outside circumstances change for the seemingly better. This can be wonderful, but any outside circumstances that are experienced and lived without this knowing of our own being will not be complete. This is why so many people who seem successful in the eyes of the world end up miserable or have ended their lives. The search for happiness in outside "things" such as money, jobs, or relationships will always fail. It's simply not possible to find lasting happiness in any element of experience. When this search for happiness "out there" is exhausted, one often finds that their internal or spiritual GPS kicks in and some event "happens" that causes them to turn inside, to seek lasting peace and happiness in the only place it can ever be found.

"The kingdom of heaven is within you."

~ JESUS, IN THE GOSPEL OF LUKE

Like the beggar who sits unknowingly on a box of gold, most people never glimpse the treasure that is the core of their very being.

α: *Why is the paradigm of our true nature never taught in our traditional educational systems?*

Ω: The common educational systems of the world are still almost completely bought in to the belief that we are separate individual entities composed of a body and mind.

Moreover, the belief is that awareness is actually a product of the brain that is "born" when the brain is "born" and will cease to exist or die when the body, and thus brain, dies. As such, most teachers of traditional education and higher "university" education believe they too are limited and finite bodies. So you see, it's impossible to teach from this expanded perspective without having the perspective for oneself. At the very least, one would need to understand this perspective as a strong possibility in order to teach it effectively.

α: *Why is this also not taught in most religious services? I attended a Catholic church for the better part of thirty years and never heard this once.*

Ω: Most of the traditional religious systems have also long ago abandoned the perennial wisdom of their foundational message, which was rooted directly in teaching the truth of our nature as the Still Point being identical with that of the transcendent. In the Old Testament of the Hebrew Bible, when God described himself as "I am that I am," it is a statement that directly points to our shared true nature. This was true wisdom and true teaching. Over time, this message was distorted to imagine God as a distant super being that is far away from our limited separate human selves to whom we must supplicate in the hope of a future, post death of the body, reunion. Thus, most religions have been reduced to belief systems propagated by power structures that use fear of future reprisal for compliance.

α: *Does this point of someone "turning around" or going inside only happen when it's clear one can't find happiness in outside objects and circumstances?*

Ω: It is unique and different for everyone. Some people have reached the seeming end of their rope, like the prodigal son, while others may not be in such dire straits, but nonetheless stumble on this teaching and become hooked.

Likewise, many people have a glimpse of their true nature of awareness in the midst of great or prolonged suffering, and realize there may be another, better way. Indeed, there are others who are not experiencing significant suffering but have a general ongoing low-level sense of being unfulfilled, dissatisfied, or tense. This can be enough to ignite the search for peace and happiness within.

α: *Is this self-knowing or the knowing of our being as awareness the end of suffering?*

Ω: Suffering is resistance to whatever one is experiencing in the moment. There can't be suffering without resistance. So, complete surrender to what is ends suffering in that moment. It's true that as we recognize ourselves as this open allowing awareness, we begin to take on its qualities in everyday life. Because the nature of awareness is acceptance of any and every experience, as we become more and more like our true nature, we see resistance and suffering drop away. This doesn't mean if we are in physical pain for example, we don't try to alleviate that pain because that's completely normal. Psychological pain or distress however become accepted completely, and this complete surrender is its own solution to the "problem."

α: *What about a general sense of unease, or a feeling that something is just not right?*

Ω: That is a subtler form of resistance to the current situation you face as well. The vast majority of the time, people who are feeling that slight sense of agitation or unrest are creating it completely in their mind by thinking unhelpful thoughts. It's actually not the thoughts themselves but rather believing the thoughts are important and must be listened too. When we find ourselves "agitated" yet are facing no external physical threat and have adequate food, water, and shelter, we are engaged in mental resistance. We are telling ourselves, sometimes subtly, that our current experience is not OK. This is a recipe for discontent as its masks the underlying peace and happiness of your true self. When this occurs, you are back to seeking happiness in the one place it can never ever be found—outside experience.

α: *This sense of agitation happens when I try to sit in meditation. What am I to do?*

Ω: It's important not to discipline the thoughts that seem to be distracting you. Rest knowingly as yourself, which is also that simple sense of being. This is not a directing of attention but rather a relaxing of attention to simply be aware of being aware. You are resting in and as your very self. If sensations arise that you previously labeled as anxiety or fear, sit with the sensations closely and do not label them with thought at all. Don't try to avoid them, but instead face them directly and completely. You will see that although they have a certain intensity to them, they are no more than vibrations in the empty field-like presence of awareness. Every time you do this, they lose a bit of their ability to pull you away from the peace of your being. In essence, you have found the dreaded horrible wizard to be nothing more than a man pulling levers behind a curtain, as the classic scene from *The Wizard of Oz* portrays.

α: *How does this understanding change the way we interact with people?*

Ω: The recognition that your being is the same as everyone's being is the feeling of love. While personalities are different, just like bodies have differences, their underlying "reality" is exactly the same being. Interactions with anyone should come from this understanding or this place of love. As Ken Wapnick, who understood and taught *A Course in Miracles* at the highest level, would say, "If people treat you with love the only appropriate response is to treat them with love. Likewise, if people treat you seemingly less than kindly, they are calling out for love. In that case the proper response is to treat them with love." This does not mean you ever condone unconsciousness or rude behavior, but always interacting with others from a place of love means you can't go wrong.

α: *It doesn't seem possible to love everyone.*

Ω: That's because your mind is thinking of people as their conditioned personality traits and not their underlying being or awareness, which is your awareness too. You love your own being, and when you see everyone as sharing that being, loving everyone is the only choice. You don't need to like or approve of everyone's personality traits, but loving everyone's core being is simply an extension of loving yourself. When this is not the case, it's because you do not yet see yourself as the Still Point of aware-being but rather you are still associating yourself with the conditioned ego, or separate self.

α: *Wouldn't this then have great implications for the peace of the world?*

Ω: Absolutely. When one recognizes their true essential nature, they recognize this freedom not as a person, but rather freedom from the idea of being a person. Meaning freedom from all the false conditioned beliefs that kept us in the bondage of believing we were a separate isolated person who is born, struggles through life, then dies. This awakening is the recognition that all of humanity is free as well. This is why the work of self-realization is the highest endeavor one can undertake.

As the great Zen master Shunryu Suzuki said,

"There are, strictly speaking, no enlightened people, there is only enlightened activity."

α: *When I meditate deeply and rest as the Still Point, it's so black and empty it can seem terrifying. It's like a void of nothingness into which I fear I will disappear. What is there to do?*

Ω: As the sixteenth century Christian mystic St. John of the Cross said, "If a man wishes to be sure of the road he treads on, he must close his eyes and walk in the dark."

He was directly referring to the necessity of going all the way back through the limited layers of mind rife with thoughts and feelings to the pure ground of awareness itself. When we do this, we find that while everything drops away, a sense of identity remains. Not a personal identity, but identity itself; we see that gloriously, we remain. We realize we are not a thing, but certainly not nothing. We are, and we see that our being can't be taken away. This is the recognition of life being eternal. This is the true freedom that transforms one's life completely. It takes courage to make this discovery because the conditioned ego mind, which you previously associated with, senses it will lose its grip and dominion over you. The ego mind wants you to fear your annihilation so much that you return to identifying with your thoughts and feelings exclusively.

It's such a cosmic joke. We fear death and disappearance, but we cling with all our sense of identity to the limited mind that is always coming and going. Our thoughts and feelings come and go constantly, never staying the same or even remaining at all in deep sleep, yet we cling to them as if they are our identity. All the while, our true ever-present nature of awareness remains always. This shift we make in identifying ourselves with this ever-present awareness shatters the illusion of being temporary, limited humans. This is the great discovery of one that frees all.

α: *It seems more and more people are turning inward to the discovery of self at this time. Is this the case?*

Ω: Yes. We are in the midst of the biggest wave of "awakening" or self-realization this planet has ever seen. In many ways, this is absolutely necessary at this time. Our unconscious living has not only created wars and famine, it has brought us to the edge of mass destruction. The earth itself has also suffered greatly from our collective human unconsciousness. Waves of people are waking up to their true nature and collectively reshaping collective human consciousness for the better. Long entrenched power structures that have held this world hostage are being dismantled before our eyes.

Despite all these external realities, our main job is for each and every one of us to turn inward and discover our unified being of unlimited awareness—the Still Point. It is with this recognition that we can play a hugely significant part in the formation of the new earth.

α: *Are the recent global events affecting this "awakening" process?*

Ω: Any event that is challenging—whether personal, nation-wide, or global—gives everyone the option to react from fear or from love. If you identify yourself strongly or completely as a limited separate human body and mind, you will likely react from fear. If you have seen clearly, or are beginning to see clearly, that you are not just a body-mind but rather the untouchable Still Point in which the body and mind is experienced, you will react from love. Needless to say, reacting from love is very powerful and has the ability to affect those around you in a very positive way.

α: *Although I recognize the Still Point of awareness, it seems very difficult to not feel like a body living in an outside world, being subject to its whims.*

Ω: You have decades of deep mental and physical conditioning to release and that does not generally happen overnight. In addition to the personal conditioning deeply driven into us by this materialist society, we all come into this world with deep collective human conditioning that we are limited body-minds as well. This is why returning to rest as awareness over and over again is necessary for most of us. It gradually frees us from the misunderstanding of being limited bodies and minds. In time, when we have "found this awareness" as what we already always were, we begin to live from this understanding. We become happy because we know that regardless of what our life circumstances seem to be, they can't affect what we truly are in any way. This allows one to surrender to whatever is, and yet if action is required it is the most useful powerful action that can be taken in that moment.

α: *When* **A Course in Miracles** *or other spiritual systems talk about the world being unreal or an illusion, which is true?*

Ω: There is something absolutely real about our experience of the world, so saying the world is not real runs the risk of being misunderstood. The world is not, however, what we have made it out to be as a solid mass of matter that exists independent of and outside awareness. This is why it is an illusion. The only reality to the world is the awareness with which it is known, and also made of. It's just not what it seems, meaning not what our conditioning has taught us to believe. Just like when you look at a movie screen you are actually seeing a unified whole that appears to be made of separate objects and separate people running around. You can't walk up to the screen and "pluck" an independent object off the screen. Likewise, when you are looking at the everyday scenes of life, the mind conceptualizes out different "things," but those seeming "things" are simply the Still Point vibrating within itself. Quantum physics has proven that so-called solid matter is 99.9999 percent space. You see, even though the jury is in, most still live under the mis-conditioned belief that the world is made of independent objects made of solid matter. That is the illusion.

α: *Is the world then seen in a new way?*

Ω: With this understanding, the world is finally seen exactly as it is without the deep "the -world-is-made-of-solid-matter" conditioning that has been drilled into us since infancy. This is what William Blake meant when he said, "If the doors of perception were cleansed everything would appear to man as it is: infinite." Here infinite means without dimensions or borders, or beyond the boundaries of space-time. The word infinite is often misunderstood to mean a space that goes on forever and ever. In fact, infinite here more accurately means "impossible to calculate" or having no borders. Because all seeming things are fundamentally made of the Still Point—which has no borders, limits, or dimensions—matter is seen as the illusion it is, as a temporary limitation that can't be limited. Thus, you are unlimited.

α: *Is it correct to say we are living in a hologram?*

Ω: We are not living in a hologram, rather the hologram-like experience we seem to be having is taking place within us—universal awareness or consciousness. When you rest as your true nature of awareness, being aware of itself, you see that all experience arises in awareness and you realize that no experience can be known without awareness. This is the way to begin to experientially understand that awareness itself is the substance of all experience. Every sight and sound, thought or feeling you have ever had is made of your very self, awareness vibrating within itself.

α: *Is there a strong element of belief needed to recognize our true nature?*

Ω: Are you interested in believing who you are or knowing who you are from direct experience? Direct experiential knowing is necessary to experience the peace and happiness that are the inherent qualities of your authentic self. Belief can only produce a fragile peace at best. This is why religious systems based on the belief in a deity at a great distance from you can at best provide a shaky peace. The only way to lasting peace and happiness is to directly know yourself as that which can't be harmed in any way and does not die.

α: *Is it necessary to have a teacher or a guru for this recognition?*

Ω: The Still Point of aware being itself is the ultimate teacher. Once you recognize this as what you really are and rest again and again as awareness, in time it reveals its ever-present unlimited nature directly. Of course, it's perfectly fine if you find a teacher who resonates with you. In this era this teaching is very available, unlike in the not-too-distant past when you had to fly to India or some other exotic locale to find a teacher established in this understanding. The place this understanding must be put to the real test is in your everyday life experiences. If life is not becoming more peaceful and enjoyable, the point is being missed.

6

THE HEALING OF OUR RELATIONSHIPS

While we have already discussed how the understanding of our true nature can radically alter our community, national, and global relationships, the first and most evident change will be seen in your personal relationships with your spouse, family, and friends. Romantic relationships, which are often the most turbulent, can be completely transformed when one or both parties come from this place of understanding. This is the difference between what *A Course in Miracles* calls a "special relationship" versus a "holy relationship." Almost all romantic relationships in which neither party has glimpsed this understanding is a "special" relationship in which one partner wants or chooses another for the purpose of making them happy by "filling in" their sense of lack. This is a recipe for disaster as witnessed by the massive rates of separation and divorce seen all over the world. The only one who can make you feel whole and complete is you. When you knowingly or unknowingly look to your partner to make you happy, you are back to looking for happiness and a sense of being complete "out there" in the world of experience, in the one place you are guaranteed never to find it. It is simply not possible, and the sooner you see this clearly, the better. When both partners are operating under this premise of expecting the other to deliver them happiness, it's only a matter of time before the initial luster of the relationship has worn off and they secretly start to blame or resent their partner. They then look to recapture this sense of satisfaction outside the relationship, with others, or simply turn to substances or sink into a routine of quiet, and at times not-so-quiet, desperation. The antidote for this is the recognition that we are already whole and complete. There is nothing that anyone could possibly add to us to make us what we already are. We are then free to enjoy holy relationships, where we no longer hold the other to the impossible task of making us happy. This is true freedom and the only way these relationships can survive and thrive over time.

α: *Is it necessary for both partners to recognize themselves as the Still Point of being or awareness for the relationship to be healed?*

Ω: Even one partner undertaking this inquiry and clearly seeing their true nature will have transformative results in their relationships. This understanding leads very clearly to one taking complete responsibility for their state of being, which means others are "off the hook" as being responsible for one's happiness. The process of gradual transformation in one partner, and the peace it brings, is often contagious, spreading to the other partner, as well as children and others in the family circle.

α: *I fear that with this understanding I will become a doormat and my partner will take advantage of my newfound passivity.*

Ω: On the contrary, a clear understanding of yourself will lead to peace but not passivity in a subservient way. It is true you will no longer react from a place of blameful anger, but you will not condone unconscious behavior on the part of your partner or anyone. From a place of greater understanding, you will be firm when needed, even to the point of moving on from the relationship if necessary. But even that will be a move made from a place of love, and not hatred or anger, making any transition much easier than it would have been under the old paradigm of being two separate warring selves.

α: *Can your spouse or partner serve as a gauge of progress as we seek this understanding of our true nature?*

Ω: They already do, whether you are aware of it or not. The quality of interactions in your personal relationships directly reflects your sense of identity. The more you are identified with a separate ego, the interactions will be turbulent and troubled with copious blame placed on the other. As your identity shifts toward the recognition that you are this unlimited awareness, these interactions become more peaceful and you begin to take full responsibility for all of your actions and reactions.

α: *Is there a way to get my spouse or partner to turn their attention to understanding their true nature?*

Ω: No one can be forced to seek this understanding, but the best way to make that happen is to be a living example of this teaching in your daily life. The aware-being that you are is open and nonreactive, accepting whatever comes into and out of experience without judgement. When you live as the awareness you are, the simple nonconfrontational peace will be apparent to your spouse or partner. This alone has the greatest effect possible on the core dynamic of the relationship. It's very possible that he or she will want that very peace for themselves and begin to question their true nature as well. If both partners are dedicated to this self-discovery, they can become a very powerful team that accelerates the understanding in each other.

α: *So, falling out of love does not happen as much?*

Ω: Love is the shared realization that what you both are (aware-being) is the same. You both share the very same being. This is not a realization that comes and goes unless one again confuses their identity with the conditioned ego self, or the realization was not complete in the first place. It's entirely possible that two people at any stage of this understanding will move apart for any number of reasons, but you can't undo the true recognition of our shared being. This applies to everyone, not just romantic partners, family, or close friends. Because people have different personalities and interests, you won't like everyone in life, but not loving everyone is not an option once your true nature of awareness is clearly seen.

α: *Why is it that relationships that start off with intense attraction often turn out to be horribly troubled in the end?*

Ω: In these relationships, we initially glimpse ourselves in the other. This early love we feel is often very intense and pleasurable, but without the knowledge that we are complete and whole, already we assign the other person the impossible task of making us happy by fulfilling our sense of lack. This is simply not possible. When it is seen that this is not possible, we turn on them and blame them for not being able to complete an impossible task. The only way out of this is for one or both parties to recognize their own sense of completion as the unlimited awareness they already are. This frees the "other" from this impossible task, and the relationship has the best chance possible to recover and flourish.

α: *What about partners with different spiritual beliefs who argue frequently about the best path to realization of self?*

Ω: Two partners arguing about what path to truth is the "best path" is much like a couple who have lived at home in Los Angeles all their lives. One day, forgetting they live in LA, they plan a road trip from New York City to LA. One wants to go via a northerly route through Chicago and the Rockies, and the other wants a more southerly route along the Gulf Coast and through the southwest. They are forgetting they are already "home" in LA dreaming they need to somehow get back to where they already always are. We are all always the Still Point of aware-being. Our home is awareness. We are awareness. In the waking state we are aware of our experiences, the sights and sounds and thoughts and feelings we have. In the dream state at night, we are aware of the dreamed characters and the dream world. In deep sleep, we are aware of being aware, with no objects or experiences to be had.

All spiritual, artistic, or scientific paths, if taken all the way, lead us to the recognition of our true self as unlimited, ever-present, self-aware being. The path is not what is ultimately important. The destination is important. The destination is the recognition that you are peace and happiness itself without modification or ending. Experiences will always come and go. Even the perspective and experiences of differing body-minds come and go, but you, awareness, already are, always.

Wake up! You appear restless in but dreams.
You fear you have traveled to a distant alien
shore, but you are completely safe at home.

α: *What about couples counseling as a substitute for this understanding?*

Ω: There are many therapists who are beginning to include this understanding into their practices, and of course that's a very positive development. While more traditional therapy approaches that come from the belief that people not only have separate personalities but also are separate beings can never be a complete solution. It's not possible for one ego to wake up to the understanding of their completion, let alone two to come together in complete harmony, while fundamentally feeling and believing they are separate. The ego is literally a point of view only, and not an actual separate entity. The dissolution of that "point of view," by clearly seeing its nonexistence or unreality, is necessary for long-term peace in relationships.

As Albert Einstein said, "We cannot solve our problems with the same level of thinking that created them." This is a beautiful way of saying that problems that arise on the level of the thinking mind, on behalf of an ego that is thought to be real, cannot be solved there. It is necessary to clearly see oneself as the awareness in which all seemingly separate minds reside. From this "level," we recognize no separate other with whom to be in conflict, and the petty arguments that served to protect and defend a separate self fade away into a newfound sense of unity and peace.

α: *Is the pursuit of romantic relationships a bad idea if you still believe in being a separate self and have not yet understood yourself to be timeless being?*

Ω: Any relationship in which the parties are looking to the other to make them happy or to complete them is built on shaky ground. But every relationship has the potential to be a tremendous personal lesson. Because people have and will enter into romantic relationships regardless of their level of understanding of their true nature, it's important for one, or ideally both partners, to see clearly their own natural completeness or wholeness. This recognition comes from the "felt understanding" that one is not just a limited body, but the Still Point of awareness in which the experience of the body and mind occurs. It can be a fantastic experience when a couple is moved to pursue this understanding together because there can be a very significant acceleration of the process of correctly integrating the understanding, once clearly seen, into their daily interactions.

α: *What do you mean by a "felt understanding" of their true nature of awareness?*

Ω: When you ask yourself the question, "Am I aware?" and you pause then clearly say yes, it is because you have the direct felt knowing that you are indeed aware. It's not a belief in being aware. You know it because it's completely obvious to you. No one else needs to tell you that you are aware. In fact, no one telling you that you are not aware would make any difference because you absolutely know you are aware of whatever experience you are having, or you wouldn't be having an experience.

α: *So, the couple helps each other with the integration of this new understanding into their daily lives, but not the understanding itself?*

Ω: All recognition is self-recognition. Because the recognition that you are actually the Still Point—and not just a limited body-mind—is a felt knowing understanding and not a belief it is entirely up to you to come to this recognition. Others can point, of course, but can never take you there directly. This recognition of yourself as an aware-being happens in an instant, a timeless instant actually, because aware-being—your true self—does not reside in space or time. Just as you are always aware, awareness or being is ever present or eternal.

After it is clearly seen and felt that you are this ever-present awareness, you will reassert this fact over and over again until the false limitations you placed on yourself when you believed you were a body begin to fade. At any point after this recognition that you are awareness, a partner can be a wonderful gauge of your progress in taking this understanding into your daily life. The result of this newfound understanding is a relationship that becomes much less judgmental and more peaceful.

α: *What is the value of a relationship between two people who still believe they are separate body-minds?*

Ω: To cause so much grief and suffering they both realize there must be a better way... [LAUGHTER] No, but there is some truth to that in the case of those who have a deep desire to make the relationship work, despite the frequent arguments and the pain. It's a well-known story that Helen Schucman, the scribe of *A Course in Miracles*, was in constant conflict with her colleague Bill Thetford when one day he implored that "there must be a better way." This led ultimately to the scribing of *A Course in Miracles* and a complete transformation of their shared relationship.

α: *Is conflict necessary for one or both parties in a relationship to "turn inward" to the recognition of our higher self?*

Ω: Conflict is a simple by-product of coming from the belief that you are a separate limited self with your own agenda that you believe has greater priority than your spouse or partner's agenda. When two people who have failed to see that they are actually exactly the same core being come together in relationship, there will be a subtle, or at times not-so-subtle, desire or need to "get your way." Remember you believe that the other person is there to "complete you" and provide your happiness. It's easy to see this sense of separation as being the root of all relationship problems. When most people come to a point of exhaustion with the constant bickering and fighting, they simply look elsewhere to solve the problem. This is why most marriages end in divorce and why people go through many serial relationships in order to find a lasting sense of fulfillment. This approach can never work. It is only when a deeper sense of commitment exists in a relationship that one recognizes the need to go within, to find the sense of completion and happiness that can only come from knowing ourselves as already complete. Relationships can then truly flourish as celebrations of this wonderful recognition.

α: *How would a more spiritually advanced culture foster the value of committed relationships? Our society certainly does not seem to do so.*

Ω: Society would encourage us to know ourselves clearly before entering into binding relationships with others. Our educational systems continually reinforce the belief that we are separate limited individuals and this teaches us that happiness can only be found by acquiring something "out there" in the world. When we view relationships as another acquisition to make us happy, we place an impossible burden on our partners. On the other hand, if our formal and familial educations emphasized the truth, that we are all the same one universal being, our relationships could flourish with this understanding. Couples would serve to continually reinforce this true understanding with each other, and the relationship would be a living ground of continual improvement.

α: *Wouldn't that necessitate widespread change to the current system?*

Ω: Yes, but imagine the possibilities of an educational system that did not force children to all learn the same flawed curriculum. By not teaching the same old materialistic paradigm that we are all separate fragile beings who must defend ourselves at all costs, we would instead teach the true unity of our one, self-aware being. By the time most were ready to enter into a long-term relationship with a partner, they would not be under the impossible delusion that the purpose of the relationship was to make them happy. Relationships would have the best possible chance of thriving and be forever changed for the better. Of course, before this can become our reality, those in the position of teaching would also need to understand, at least to some tangible level, that they too are this one unified being or awareness at their core.

THE SAFETY OF YOUR
TRUE NATURE

The recognition that you are aware is self-evident to any person, or indeed to any sentient being. Simply by asking yourself the question, "Do I feel I am?" or "Am I aware?" results in an undeniable yes. This is the sense of "I" that everyone has and knows so well. What is not as evident is then going beyond the almost continual stream of thinking to see what the true, inherent qualities of yourself are, what you call "I," and what that fully encompasses. In a sense, this is the "hard part," or the work of self-discovery. It's one thing to recognize that you are an aware-being, but what does that really mean and how can it make your experience of life more joyful? This is why meditation is so central to so many religious and spiritual systems. The world has recognized the value of meditation for stress reduction, as well as to improve many aspects of health. If meditation is so widespread, why is the recognition that we are ever-present, unlimited awareness not more widely known? True meditation is strikingly simple, but the thinking mind rushes in with widespread, distracting thoughts. The problem is not actually the thoughts, but the fact that we associate ourselves with those very thoughts. We allow those thoughts to generate more thoughts and the feelings that accompany them to "carry us away." This is why it's very important to see directly that you are not your thoughts, but the silent awareness from which those thoughts arise and into which they dissipate. True meditation is resting as awareness, simply aware of itself. It's a complete non-doing. From this place, one is able to see that awareness is completely open and unchanging. It has no judgement of any thoughts or feelings that arise within it. It's that unchanging aspect of everyone's experience. When you get in touch with the feeling of "I" that we all have, you recognize it's exactly the same unchanging sense of "I" as when you were five or ten years old. Your thoughts and feelings change all the time, but not the deep, always present sense of "I." Of course, even bodies change over time, but what you truly are, the sense of aware-being known as "I" is unchangeable. There is very little that one can say about awareness or the sense of "I." In truth, it is an indescribable, formless presence but it is undeniably always present and aware. Without it, no sight would ever be seen, and no sound would ever be heard. Thinking and feeling would be impossible. This is your very self and it has been overlooked by most people for their entire lives. Meditation is resting knowingly as the awareness you are, so it can reveal, in a felt knowing way, its indestructible, ever-present reality.

α: *I have been meditating off and on for a few years, using a mantra to focus on, but it doesn't feel like life is becoming more peaceful. What is to be done?*

Ω: In his notebook J. Krishnamurti said, "Without self-knowing all meditation leads to delusion and to varying forms of self-deception. The many systems of meditation merely trap the mind in a pattern offering marvelous escapes and sensations; it is only the immature that play with them, getting a great deal of satisfaction from them." The point Krishnamurti was making here is when meditation tries to transcend the mind by exclusively using the mind, the risk of getting trapped or stuck in the thinking mind is great. This is why establishing yourself as the Still Point, the ground of aware-being, when you sit to meditate is critical. Even if using a repetitive mantra, which is nothing more than a thought represented by a sound in the mind, it's the space between thoughts that is important. When you want to see the open sky, you don't focus exclusively on a cloud, you can let clouds come and go as they please.

α: *What is the value of words in guided meditations? Should silence not suffice?*

Ω: The words are only pointers to the silence, which is their source. In a skillful guided meditation, the words are not being directed to the filtering mechanism of the ego mind, but to your deeper being. As such, the words are not meant to be scrutinized by your intellect, but rather to continually point you back to yourself. Just like there is nothing to the passing clouds but the infinite sky, there is nothing to the sound of the words but your aware being that knows them.

α: *Is there a point when meditation becomes effortless?*

Ω: Meditation, or being aware of being aware, is effort-lessness itself; it is not something you do. All thoughts arise from awareness and seem to move out or away from awareness to an object of some sort. This is why meditation seems to be hijacked by constant chattering thoughts so often. Let the thoughts come and go without the slightest attachment to them, and they will eventually fall back into their source. Meditation is not a focusing of attention, but a relaxing of attention. If you focus your attention on the content of thoughts, you will be inexorably pulled away from the ground of your aware-being.

α: *Then meditation is not something that happens only when one sits in silence?*

Ω: In the purest essence, meditation is what you are: timeless being. The idea of a separate person sitting to meditate is a concession to the incorrect belief in separation, yet of course it's natural to speak of it in this way while the belief in separation still exists. Meditation, as the act of knowingly being your ever-present aware self, does not end in the face of bodily activity or "moving through the world." On the contrary, it's the unbroken act of remaining your peaceful, open self, regardless of what activity you are undertaking. True meditation does not have the sense of one who is meditating on something; it's the collapse back into the only thing that really is, the Still Point of your aware-being.

α: *Can one come to awakening or enlightenment without the formal practice of sitting in meditation?*

Ω: Awakening is knowing yourself as the one self or being of all beings, and knowing experientially the unlimited, ever-present nature of that being. Anyone can come to this recognition at any time, but for most, this only becomes a "living reality" after a serious period of self-contemplation, of which meditation is often a part. Even for those who have followed more "outward-facing or devotional paths," a time of turning inward, away from fixation on thoughts and sensations, is usually necessary.

α: *Is there an optimal time to meditate?*

Ω: The optimal time to meditate is when it is the most enjoyable or exciting thing to do at that time. It's perfectly understandable given the hectic schedules of many to set aside some time daily, but in truth, many will find the most effective meditations are those that happened spontaneously out of a deep desire to meditate in that moment. All desire ultimately comes from your true being, so when the desire for stillness arises, it should be followed.

α: *Is there a greater power in group meditations versus meditating alone?*

Ω: The recognition of your unlimited nature as the Still Point is self-recognition alone. It's true that groups dedicated to this understanding, who are meditating under the guidance of one established in this understanding, often have a deep transformative power to spark this recognition, but it remains the job of everyone alone to see this clearly. So, by all means, meditating in the presence of those who share this understanding can be helpful, but is certainly not necessary.

α: *You said, "All desire comes from our true being." Can you elaborate?*

Ω: Every desire we have is ultimately a desire for contentment, or happiness. We get so caught up in the intermediary objects, we think that we desire them in and of themselves, which is never true. For example, if you desire a particular job, it's not the actual job that is desired but the happiness we think it will bring us. It's the same with the car we desire, or the relationship, or having more money. If we knew that any one of those objects would not bring us happiness or contentment, we would drop it immediately. Our true nature is happiness itself, so all desire is a pull from ourselves to ourselves. To know ourselves as we are is contentment itself. From this place of understanding, any of these objects can be enjoyed greatly for what they are, but we no longer give them the impossible task of causing our happiness.

α: *I was raised a Roman Catholic and then read* **A Course in Miracles,** *which came as a very welcome relief as a reinterpretation of the teachings of the Church. The Course talks constantly of the Holy Spirit, what is the relationship of the Holy Spirit to the Still Point in this direct approach?*

Ω: Whole spirit or Holy Spirit is the ground of being shared by us all. It is whole, meaning it is complete and lacks nothing. It was not born and will not die. It never comes and goes and cannot be hurt in any way. Spirit is its formless nature that has no objective qualities but is always present and knowing. Holy Spirit is what we are referring to as the Still Point of aware-being. The simple awareness with which we are reading these words. One can use the words Awareness, Knowing, Being, the Still Point, Holy Spirit, Christ consciousness, Buddha nature, the Tao, or even what we all call "I," the list goes on and on, all referring to exactly the same thing.

α: *The message of Jesus then was ultimately pointing to finding the truth within us all as the way to freedom?*

Ω: The person of Jesus was a radical spiritual revolutionary of his time. If you read the Gospels through the lens of this understanding, you can see his message was powerfully direct, pointing people to the truth dwelling within them. Of course, many parts of his message were later altered or removed to suit the power structures of the day.

Ask yourself the question, can anyone know God without first knowing themselves? It's impossible to know God and not know yourself and impossible to know yourself and not know God.

8

BE THE ACTOR AND NOT THE CHARACTER IN THE MOVIE OF LIFE

When you watch a movie, you enjoy it because you know that you are not actually subject to the fate of the characters in the movie. Imagine watching a movie where you were so completely identified with one or more of the characters that you believed what happened to them in the movie would actually affect you. Movie night would turn from being a carefree, fun experience into one filled with a low level of underlying anxiety or worry that some dreadful ill would befall you. Your fears would be well justified given the extreme violence we see on the screen today. You would never want to enter the movie as a character in the movie; it would be too stress provoking. Yet this is exactly how most people are living their lives, believing completely in the role of the character of the person they are playing in life. Believing they are only the name and form society has taught them to be. We are taught, and deeply believe, that we are bodies whose brain produces our consciousness or ability to know and be aware. We go through life with varying degrees of anxiety and fear because we believe we are at the mercy of outside events that can attack us, and when the body and brain are damaged enough, our consciousness will fade and disappear. It's literally no wonder why life, for many, is a continual effort to protect themselves from the imminent danger of attack and death. This is a horrible way to live. At best, limited periods of happiness are experienced in between long stretches of fear and worry about the future. For some, there is a constant low-level tread of "edginess" that accompanies every waking hour, with relief only seen during deep sleep. Much of humanity spends a significant portion of their time and effort trying to distract themselves from this nearly constant inner turmoil. The number of people who take antianxiety medicine or antidepressants in the developed world is at unprecedented levels. In addition, the overuse of alcohol and other drugs as tools for stress relief remains prevalent throughout society.

But what if there exists a better way to approach the "movie of life" than thinking and feeling like a character in the show? Take the actor who plays the part of a character in the show. She arrives on the set and plays the part of the character without ever being subject to the fears and worries of the character. Indeed, even if the plot sees the character attacked or injured in the movie, she simply sheds the role and goes home to her life. This is very much the experience of everyday life when it is lived from the Still Point of aware-being that you really are, at all times and under all circumstances. When you see clearly that you are this awareness, and you act from this awareness, you approach the movie of life fearlessly and can engage in its events fully and with maximum effectiveness. You resist no experience but rather merge fully with it. Your actions and responses are no longer coming from a mixed place of fear and love, but love alone. You take actions spontaneously that have in mind the best interests of everyone in your experience, and because of this they benefit you maximally as well. You can live life as the limited fearful character or the unlimited free actor. The choice at that level is always up to you.

α: *How do I take the approach of being the actor in the movie of life instead of the character?*

Ω: You will act as what you feel and know yourself to be in your experience. The freedom and flow of the actor come from moving through life as the Still Point of aware-being. This means your identification of self has shifted from the conditioned belief in being a temporary, limited person to the expanded perspective of knowing you are the unlimited and open awareness in which experience occurs, fundamentally free from annihilation by that experience.

α: *What happens to the actor when the character dies?*

Ω: The temporary form of the body dissolves and the actor, the Still Point of aware being, is freed from the limitations associated with a limited form. This becomes evident when you return to rest as awareness over and over again. You see it has been changeless for your entire life regardless of the experiences you have had. It takes a shift of focus from the near continuous interest in our thoughts and feelings to that which makes thinking and feeling possible.

α: *But my experiences have never included death.*

Ω: Every single night when you fall asleep, your experience of the body and your personal identity drops away completely. In dreams, the mind creates a new world and seems to project you as a character into that world so you can experience it much like you do in the waking state. You, awareness, remain to be aware of the dream state and the dreamed character. Likewise, in deep sleep there are no things to be aware of, so awareness remains aware of itself. This is why it is so enjoyable.

α: *When we act as the character in the movie of life, and not the actor, are we operating from the ego self?*

Ω: Yes, but there is no "self" or independent existence of something called an ego. It is nothing but a thought system to which you have willingly given over your power by believing in it alone. The only true "self" of the character in the movie is the actor who plays the role. The character's mind does not exist in and of itself. It is only the actor's mind that has willingly taken on the conditioning that belongs to the character. When you see clearly that the character's fears and anxieties were overlaid on the clear and free mind of the actor, which is the only mind that exists, you can discard the "point of view" of the character in favor of the actor simply playing a role. Over time, the constriction of this false, nonexistent self diminishes and dissipates, and freedom is regained.

α: *The character can then return as another character after death in a reincarnation?*

Ω: The character never existed in the first place so that which does not "incarnate" can't "reincarnate." The actor is the only "truth" to the character and indeed the actor, which is unlimited awareness or being, can play the role of many characters. It is not the character jumping from role to role, but the actor alone.

α: *People often seem to remember past lives though.*

Ω: Yes, because the actor who has previously played the role of a certain character in a movie, who is now playing another role years later, can remember aspects of a previous role, at times. If you are an actor who played the part of John F. Kennedy in a movie ten years ago and today are playing a role as a different person, you could well have memories of the "life" of JFK. If you believe you are the character now, and not the actor playing the role, you will believe you were the previous character who has reincarnated. You see the error is right up front. When you believe you are a person with an independent existence and seem to have a past life memory, the mind can only assume that you, the person then, has become you, the person now. In reality when you see clearly that you are the Still Point of aware-being, and the idea of a person is only a role being played, it becomes clear that only awareness is the common linking factor.

α: *We hear a lot about the coming advances in artificial intelligence (AI) and how this will eventually lead to the destruction of the human race. Can you comment on this a bit?*

Ω: Technology itself is almost never the problem but rather the thought system that conceives of and deploys the technology is the issue. In essence, we are looking at the "problem" in the wrong way. Any technology managed and driven by the ego thought system of separation and fragmentation will, if taken to its natural end, result in either partial or complete destruction. It is a universal law. On the other hand, we can speculate and conceive of very advanced civilizations, perhaps millions of years beyond earth currently, that have integrated such technologies in a very helpful way. Those civilizations would have long prior made the necessary collective shift from the thought system of the ego to the realization of our joint conscious being. In other words, from fear to love or separation to unity. If this was not achieved, such a civilization would have likely destroyed itself long ago. Earth itself has now long passed the point where our destructive capability has far outstripped our collective spiritual mass. This is why the current wave of mass awakening on this planet is so very critical.

α: *Is this work of recognizing oneself as the Still Point considered self-help? Is the ego worth studying?*

Ω: It's self-discovery and not self-help because the self that we are pointing to needs no help. When the self is truly known it is known as the self of all, eternally present and without the slightest resistance to what is. The Still Point is intelligent infinity in which all relational knowledge is known, but never held. As far as the ego, if you feel compelled to study it, by all means do so, but never believe it is you again. For most, living to serve the demands and absurd dictates of the ego brings enough suffering to only desire transcendence from it, and not further understanding of it, but each is different.

α: *Does transcendence of the ego not eliminate the mind completely?*

Ω: It stills the mind so creative intelligence can flow through, but it does not eliminate the aspect of the filtering system that has been configured through education and learning. One needs a baseline of conceptual knowledge to operate in the world or you wouldn't know the difference between the functions of a chair and an automobile, for instance.

α: *But then access to all creative intelligence is available?*

Ω: What is expressed by language can only be expressed through the filtering system of the mind, no matter how "clear" or purified it may be. For example, if you are only a native Spanish speaker it's unlikely that after the recognition and establishment as the Still Point you will begin to speak fluent Russian. The only true language of God is silence. The translation into words comes through the mind that has certain filters that have been learned. Language is clearly one.

Life is a magnificent play with
innumerable characters and but one actor
who plays them all.

THE WORLD IS
A REFLECTION OF
HUMANITY'S
INNER STATE

To say we are living in turbulent times would be an understatement. Many people are waking up to the fact that the world we live in is not what we thought. We are seeing the corruption of the ego thought system reflected in many of our long-standing political, financial, and religious institutions. The desire for activism to help change the world can be a noble effort, but without first changing our minds about the world, those efforts will be limited at best. The state of the world is a direct reflection of humanity's collective inner state. Despite the fact that it has been nearly a century since many of the brightest scientists of the day seriously called into question the materialistic paradigm of matter existing outside of consciousness, we still, collectively, believe in it wholeheartedly. As the great quantum physicist Niels Bohr said, "Everything we call real is made of things that cannot be regarded as real." He was speaking directly to the fact that what we call "solid" matter is not solid, nor does it exist in the way we once imagined. Most people still believe they are small insignificant "blips" of consciousness that somehow, despite the fact no one has ever explained how, arose from dead, inert matter. This "hard problem of consciousness" aside, most people trudge on believing and acting as if they are separate limited entities that must fight to protect themselves and their interests at all costs. The expansion of this faulty and inaccurate thought system has long ago reached the limits of its usefulness and if we as a species and planet are to continue, it must be abandoned or we risk self-imposed destruction. There is one way to reverse this insidious trend, and as much as some would like to believe, it's not to fight our way to a new society but to transform society by transforming ourselves, one person at a time. When we turn our attention inward to the recognition of the Still Point of aware-being as our very nature, we awake from the matrix of an objective consensus reality. We see that the aware-being we are is everyone's shared being, and this alone has a profound effect on stirring this very recognition in others. When Gandhi said "be the change you want to see in the world," he recognized this reality clearly. The cumulative effect on collective human consciousness from the self-realization of a few can snowball into the waking of the many, or at least enough of the many, to forever change the trajectory of this planet and the human race from darkness to light.

*Think of the world as a mirror when you
smile in the mirror you are smiled upon. When
you frown you are frowned upon. Show the
mirror anger and rage and anger and
rage are all you will see.*

α: *Why do some with so much wealth and power still want
to control the masses?*

Ω: No one operating as such has any true wealth or power.
At best they have the illusion of power, but they are ignoring
the only recognition that can make them truly wealthy and
powerful—the felt understanding that they are the deathless
and inherently complete Still Point of being. There is no
power at all in the feeling of lack or the fear of extinction
at death.

α: *But they are responsible for so much oppression.*

Ω: Society is responsible for society's children. The attempt
to control is done out of fear and not love. We all must look
at ourselves and see how we have directly contributed to
these mistaken beliefs by trying to exert control in relationships, and over circumstances in general. We have little right
to be surprised when others do the same at a greater level.
The imperative we all have is to make the seeming effort to
realize the effortless Still Point that unites us all as one limitless being. From this vantage point above the battlefield of
experience, we come always from a place of love. This and
this alone has the true power of transformation needed by a
deeply wounded world.

α: *We have seen so much fear being pumped into humanity from seemingly every direction lately. It can get overwhelming. What is one to do?*

Ω: Ask yourself what is it that knows or is aware of this feeling of fear? This returns you to the self-aware Still Point that is forever unchanging. Ask yourself the further question, once you have "re-recognized" this placeless place of awareness that is the core of your very being: Has the Still Point of awareness ever been overwhelmed? You will see that it has not. The Still Point, your very self, has never been overwhelmed. It is only thinking that tells you differently. Where should you place your trust? In thoughts that constantly come and go, lasting seconds at best, or in that aspect of you that has never changed or disappeared, and which you can verify in your direct experience with a simple question and relaxation of all attention?

As to the external sources of fearful information, whether TV news or newspapers and news outlets online, no one is compelling you to give them any attention but yourself. There is no reason to overconsume information coming from a place of separation and fear, whose only real agenda is to continue the lines of political, racial, and international division. Learn what you absolutely need to know for practical purposes and move on. The ego self is nothing but false beliefs and beliefs are nothing but thoughts you think over and over again. There is no need to continually subject yourself to the false programming of an ego driven agenda.

α: *But the mind is so complex and multilayered and the ego is so deeply embedded, it seems impossible to root it out.*

Ω: The mind is nothing but thoughts and images, and images are neutral without thoughts that assign positive or negative values to them. So, you see there is nothing to what you are calling mind other than thinking. Even the subconscious and deep unconscious layers of mind are nothing but thoughts and images that one does not have ready access too. What you call ego is the mistaken belief that you are these thoughts and the feelings that accompany them. When you see clearly that you are not your thoughts and feelings but instead the vast awareness in which they appear, they have no hold over you anymore. Your problem is a simple problem of misidentification.

α: *Don't memories of traumatic events also contribute to fear?*

Ω: Memories are nothing but thoughts about what you call the past that you are having in the now. What you call trauma is a residual contraction felt in the mind, and/or the body, in the form of thoughts and feelings. Fear is only possible when you recall the past and project the future. There can be no fear when living only in the now.

α: *When you say fear can't be experienced in the now, isn't our experience always experienced now, at least when we are having it?*

Ω: Yes, absolutely, and that is a great thing to deeply contemplate. You have never experienced something called a past or a future because any experience you have ever had is always felt as happening now. Without thought you can't recall a past or imagine a future. The concept of time does not exist without thinking. There can be no fear without thinking, and when you see clearly that you are not your thoughts, fear begins to lose its grip. This, of course, is not to say "fear" that motivates in the now is not perfectly appropriate. If a tiger is chasing you, the "fear" you feel in the body that compels you to run is appropriate. It's psychological fear without any immediate threat that is the vast majority of fear that is experienced and not necessary.

α: *Then fear has no actual substance?*

Ω: The substance of fear is love. If you go deeply enough into fear, you will find only love because love is the substance of all seeming things. This is why unpleasant sensations must not be avoided, but rather looked at very closely. When fear arises, pay no attention to any accompanying thoughts but rather focus attention on the sensations that are arising in the field of awareness. You will find a familiar vibration that is constantly in slight flux. This is usually felt in the chest or stomach area, but with your eyes closed, it is just appearing within the Still Point of awareness. When you add no thought to this vibration, you see it is neutral. It does not even approach the intensity of a regular sensation of actual pain. It is thinking that takes a harmless sensation and seems to amplify it into a panicky state. When you decouple thinking from sensing, you break the vicious cycle and are able to recognize that the sensations that previously incited panic are benign and harmless. You can do this again and again when these sensations arise, and over time, they will lose their fearful associations.

α: *What is the relationship between the Still Point and love?*

Ω: They are identical. The Still Point of aware-being is felt as love in relation to people and animals. It is the experience of beauty in relation to objects of perception such as artwork, nature scenes, or music, and the experience of truth in relation to thought.

α: *Meditating and the glimpses of my true nature have helped me so much during the recent quarantine that I want my friends and family to see there is a better way than just to give in to the constant fear that is being pumped into us from the media. What is the best way to introduce this teaching as a possibility?*

Ω: You can be a living demonstration of the recognition of truth you have had. Your peace of mind and the ease with which you live will be a powerful attractor to others of the peace of the Still Point that is in them, but has yet to be glimpsed or recognized. In fact, this is the only way to demonstrate this to anyone who has not yet "turned around" and begun to question all of their beliefs. If someone has direct interest and asks why you seem to have found such peace, by all means, feel free to explain to them what you have discovered and point them in the direction of this self-discovery. If they have not yet begun to question their beliefs, attempting to lead them to this truth may cause more harm than good. Their belief structures are not yet ready to yield to deep questioning, and the fear that will arise from prematurely attempting to bring them down can be very counterproductive to awakening. Demonstration of this recognition through the way you live will be the most powerful and helpful way to transmit the possibility of a more peaceful way of living to others.

α: *It's difficult to see my family suffering needlessly from being in a constant state of fear. Fear that was seemingly forced into them from the outside that is now being amplified by their own negative thoughts.*

Ω: The choice of responding to anything from a place of love or fear is exclusively the responsibility of the individual's mind. If one has done the work of self-inquiry and begun to question the deep-conditioned beliefs that most everyone on this planet has been exposed to, then the introduction of new outside psychological fears will have no lasting hold. When we have yet to begin the inquiry into our real nature we are coming from a place of separation, which is inherently fearful. The state of being you exist as determines the thought system you employ. A state of separation is a state of isolation in which people and the world are seen as potentially hostile "others." In the state of living with the consistent recognition that you are the Still Point of aware-being, everything is recognized as self. The thoughts that arise from these respective states of being differ wildly, and directly reflect the underlying belief in separation or unity. This is why the recognition that you are the Still Point, and not your thoughts and feelings, is the place from which this investigation can truly begin. After this is initially seen, there will still be unconscious conditioned reactions to certain circumstances that seem to bring up fear, but in time, as this realization deepens, less and less has the power to pull you away from your understanding.

α: *It seems the real worry is what our minds do after we have ingested some outside fearful news or disturbing information. Perseverating and such. Is this true?*

Ω: Yes, the concepts of outside and inside need to be discarded and seen to be false because in reality, it's all inside mind. From the standpoint of one who sees and feels themselves as an isolated person, their thoughts and feelings are "inside" but the world and others are "outside." This is where the concept of "outside" influences comes from and why they often seem fearful. From one standing as the Still Point of awareness, everything arises in and is known by awareness, including what previously were felt to be "outside" perceptions. This creates a growing shift in identity away from complete immersion in patterns of thinking and feeling toward the awareness that knows them but is never affected by them in any way.

α: *It's hard to see or envision the world as inside the mind because it feels outside.*

Ω: Every night when you fall asleep you lose all sense of the body you have in the waking state. In dreams there is nothing but mind, and mind creates a new "world" and a "body" from which you seem to view the world. It's very clear to see if you really contemplate that there is nothing to this dream state but mind. There is no real physical body and no real outside world, despite the fact that it feels very much like they exist, just as in the waking state. The only changeless aspect that remains from the waking state into the dream state is the awareness with which you know both. You are this awareness, and both the experiences of these states takes place inside you, awareness. There is much to learn from the dream state, as well as deep sleep if one pays attention.

α: *Is this where the experience of lucid dreaming comes from?*

Ω: There is no lasting freedom from just the recognition that one is dreaming, if they refer "reality" back to being a separate isolated person in the waking state. It can certainly be enjoyable to know the dream is just a dream and there is a certain limited freedom in that, but real freedom lies in the recognition of lucid waking, where one has recognized their unchanging nature of aware-being while in the waking state. Living life from and as this awareness deepens over time and eventually it becomes clear there is no interruption in awareness from waking to dream, or in deep sleep. In deep sleep, because the mind is not present, it shouts upon waking, "There was nothing there," when it should say simply, "I, as mind, was not there." Just because there were no thoughts or feelings, sights or sounds, to be experienced in deep sleep, awareness remains as being aware of itself. The deeper "I" remains present and aware. This is why deep sleep is such a peaceful and enjoyable non-experience. Have you ever known anyone who does not love deep sleep? Again, this, like the dream state, is something to deeply contemplate. It can give many answers.

α: *Can you say more about the two "I's" of the mind and of the deeper self?*

Ω: There is only one "I." What you and everyone has called "I" your entire life is the Still Point of aware-being that has been ceaselessly present and aware of any and all experience you have ever had. When you mix this "I" of pure awareness with thoughts, feelings, and other experiences, you seem to create the little "I." This is the "I" of limitation in which you have mistakenly identified yourself with temporal things that come and go all the time. This is the reason for anxiety, fear, anger, and all the negative emotional states you have ever experienced. Instead of your mind recognizing itself as a natural function of ever-present awareness, it believes that it is your reality, and being a temporary limited thing, it is terrifying. The way out of this dilemma is to free awareness from the crushing limitation that arises from mixing its pure, completely accepting nature with limited aspects of experience that come and go all the time. The pure "sky" of awareness is stripped from the belief that it was the passing clouds, and now returns to its ever-present self. Clouds can come and go without ever affecting the sky just as thoughts and feelings can come and go without ever affecting the underlying Still Point of aware-being that is the "real" you.

α: *What more can be said of the Still Point?*

Ω: In truth, nothing can be said about it at all. Because it has no objective qualities, words do not apply. While it can't be known in the way we know objects, all objects such as sights, sounds, thoughts, and feelings are known in it and by it alone. You are the Still Point that makes all experience possible but itself is not an experience. Just as the screen on which the movie plays is not itself featured in the movie, there could also be no movie without the screen. The only "reality" to the movie is the screen just as the only reality to any experience is the Still Point of awareness with which it is known.

α: *Isn't taking action to improve the state of the world more effective in actually helping the world than only meditating or contemplating our own being?*

Ω: The greatest blessing any being can offer the world is to recognize the Still Point of awareness as your very self. In this recognition it is seen that it is the very self of all beings, as well as the "substance" of the world appearance. Any action that you then take from this understanding will have far more intrinsic value then actions taken from a belief in separate people and an outside solid world. Because all beings share the same ground of being, this recognition in one affects all in profound ways. Of course, serving others in a loving way is a good thing regardless of one's level of understanding, but the recognition of one's true nature as the Still Point should be prioritized. Once this recognition has occurred, it will be very clear what actions should be taken or not taken in the world to have the maximum beneficial effect.

α: *If the world reflects humanity's inner state, then the collective inner state of mankind must be pretty bleak.*

Ω: We have long ago reached the point on earth where our technological evolution has far outpaced our spiritual evolution, which is a state that can only stand for so long until we either finally destroy ourselves, or we wake up as a race. Despite the collective insanity of the previous century—with its world wars, vast political purges that killed millions, and atomic arms races—we have continued into this new century with the same insanity. This is what happens when the vast majority of people in the world are "asleep" to our collective nature of self-aware being. Love can only flow from the recognition that we are all the very same being, just having slightly different viewpoints, which is what this human experience is meant to be. The vast majority of so-called leaders, who are meant to guide nations wisely, also completely believe they are separate, isolated selves at the mercy of "others" who want to take away what they have amassed. Is it any wonder our collective actions have been so damaging? We have already passed the point where this can't continue, and in fact, it's now imperative that we, as a species, wake up to our true nature if we are to survive.

α: *Wont it take a very long time for everyone on our planet to wake up to the truth of our one shared being?*

Ω: It only takes a very small percentage who have directly understood this truth to literally change the world. Regardless, this is a revolution of one—the one being you. The only one you can ever bring to this recognition is yourself. When you recognize that you are the Still Point of being, which can't be harmed and does not die, you will have profound effects on those around you just by the nature of your being. We are all this very same being and everyone wants to recognize this more than anything else, whether they know it or not. Everyone wants to be happy, and there can be no lasting happiness without this recognition because the Still Point is happiness itself.

α: *Do outside circumstances change with the recognition of our true nature of aware presence?*

Ω: Outside circumstances may change drastically or they may not change at all, depending on their resonance with your current state of being. Many, if not most, of the so-called problems humans have are created by the constant movement of the egoic mind. As is said in *A Course in Miracles*, the ego's imperative is to "seek but never find." It is truly the ultimate fool's game where a nonexistent entity that is taken to be one's self continually looks for happiness in the only place it can never be found—in the objects and experiences of the world (relationships, substances, money, sex, power, status, etc.). Once one recognizes themselves as the untouchable Still Point of being, the ego is clearly seen to be unreal. At this point, the long-established patterns of belief enforced by egoic rule begin to subside, and along with them the lifelong contractions in the body and the mind.

10

THE RISK OF THE SPIRITUAL EGO

Until the ego is clearly seen as false, it can seem to undergo a seemingly infinite number of "mutations" in order to remain as our self-identity. Just like bacteria subject to certain powerful antibiotics will acquire resistance mechanisms in order to survive, the ego will do exactly the same. This is perhaps most evident in the concept of the "new spiritual ego." At some point, when it is recognized that seeking happiness "out there" in the objects of the world does not work, many will begin to turn inward as the last resort. This "turning around" is a critical point that everyone must reach in order to clearly see the ultimate unreality of the ego mind. This is the point in the story of the prodigal son where he turns around and begins the seemingly long journey back to the father. At this point, before the recognition of self as the Still Point of awareness, the ego gladly co-ops the search in order to "wake up" or achieve liberation itself. Although the ego mind cannot grasp the unity of the Still Point, it intuits that there is "something" bigger than itself, and to the ego this is initially both intriguing and confusing. As such, the ego gladly joins the search, at least until the investigation begins to approach the Still Point, where the ego begins to respond with intense fear and terror as it sees its imminent dissolution. While this is a very natural part of the seeming evolutionary spiritual process, it can also be a place where one gets stuck. This is where the search for happiness "out there" can subtly change into the search for happiness in exotic states of mind and experiences that can come from various forms of spiritual practice. You will often hear people talk about their Samadhi experiences and other blissful states they have attained. These can indeed be wonderful experiences, but should ultimately be seen as pleasant side effects of the beginnings of a deeper realization; namely that the real self lies beyond the limits of the thinking mind. This is the point where one needs deep humility and radical truthfulness. If one's day-to-day living is not becoming more peaceful and inclusive, there remains honest work to be done. This recognition of our true nature is not meant to be an intellectual understanding but rather a profound transformation of our daily lived experience. Understanding you are unlimited awareness and living as unlimited awareness are two very different things. The history of this world is littered with false teachers and outright cult leaders who have taken glimpses of truth and added them to their "egoic arsenal" of deception and control. Anyone who is genuine will steadfastly point others only to the discovery of this truth within themselves and never try to use the understanding to control or manipulate.

α: *I have been meditating and contemplating the nature of what I call "I" and waiting for a "breakthrough" or "sign" of progress. Is this counterproductive?*

Ω: The answer to this question was given by Jesus in the Gospel of Luke, when having been questioned by the Pharisees as to when the kingdom of God was coming, he answered them and said, "The kingdom of God is not coming with signs to be observed."

Any experience, no matter how blissful or wonderful, is known by and happens within the Still Point of awareness, which you are. This is the recognition that liberates you from the tyranny of identification with the egoic mind and the feelings generated by its insane thought system. Any blissful sensations or states of mind are perfectly fine as long as they are not seen as the goal of your investigation, but simply pleasant side effects. Many people have spent their whole lives chasing pleasure and avoiding pain which has kept them spinning on the wheel of duality. Just as unpleasant sensations and feelings must be fully faced and accepted to see their ultimate reality, the same is true of the pleasant ones.

α: *Why does the ego "mutate" as you say, to avoid being dissolved?*

Ω: The so-called ego is searching for peace as well. It desperately wants to relax by dissolving into its source, but it doesn't know this at first. For almost everyone, the ego must come to its own highest understanding before it can transcend its deep fear and fully merge with its source, which is the Still Point. Our identity with the ego is so deeply conditioned that we fear when the ego is clearly seen as nonexistent and dissolves, we too will dissolve and disappear. In reality, when everything is taken away, including the body and the thinking mind, we still "are present" as this indescribable Still

Point of aware-being. This is why the recognition is so deeply liberating. This is the point where one remembers they are the actor and not the character in the movie of life. At this point one starts to live life as awareness, and not a limited body-mind, and life becomes progressively more peaceful and happier.

α: *I came to the direct path from* **A Course in Miracles** *and the direct approach seems to ignore the ego, while* **A Course in Miracles** *seems to deal with it almost exclusively. Why is this the case?*

Ω: Every teaching is meant to meet those who come to it exactly where they currently are in terms of their understanding. *A Course in Miracles* is a beautiful psychospiritual work of non-duality. It is written with language and symbolism consistent with the Judeo-Christian tradition and very often speaks to those who were conditioned negatively by those religions in their current form. It restores the purity of Jesus's actual message, as well as the profoundly deep understanding that lies at the inception of Judaism as well. It is written to meet those whose identity is believed to be the body-mind. It progressively exposes the ego thought system as nonexistent and offers the Holy Spirit as the real alternative. Holy Spirit is another name for the Still Point of awareness.

The direct approach takes one directly to the recognition that they are the Still Point of aware-being. When this is seen, the ego is recognized as nothing but a construct given a reality that it does not have. In both approaches, the long-standing egoic conditioning must be dissolved to experience life as it is meant to be—peaceful and happy. Once someone has reached the point of turning around or inward, or as The Course puts it, the "little willingness" to question all previously held beliefs in the search for happiness and fulfillment, whatever "path" or approach is right for them will appear. If you are reading this, and have gotten this far, then you are very likely ready for a direct approach.

α: *More people than ever seem to be exploring their true nature, but how do they find the best path for them?*

Ω: It is ultimately an act of grace that simply means your true nature of aware-being presents itself to you in exactly the form you need. Whether the invitation is accepted or not is up to the individual. For some, a book will somehow appear that catches their eye, or a friend may introduce one to a teacher that resonates with them. It can happen in any number of ways but there is usually a hint of excitement that this "feels right" at the time. Whatever approach one adopts, if taken to its ultimate conclusion, it will result in the realization that there never was a "path" because you are already standing as the Still Point of awareness, but that truth has been covered up and obscured by a deep identification with thoughts and feelings. The real key is taking the teaching all the way until your questions are answered and there is a deep felt understanding of your true nature of peace and happiness.

α: *Is there ever a time or reason to switch spiritual paths?*

Ω: When one has reached the point of turning inward and the "search" for happiness in the only place it can be found has earnestly begun, it can look like anything externally. When a particular path or approach is chosen out of love, it is best to take it as far as possible. As always, the spiritual GPS will resolutely lead one where they need to go. If a change is needed because of stagnation or the inability to grasp the bigger picture, it will become very obvious if one is committed to following their heart. I have met many people who have gone from various progressive approaches, such as mantra meditation or *A Course in Miracles*, to the direct approach for various reasons. I have also met some who have taken *A Course in Miracles* all the way to the clearly felt and lived understanding of self-realization. The limitation is in the student and not the teaching, but the goal can be reached in any myriad of ways.

α: *So, following the heart is key?*

Ω: Always.

α: **On one hand you say there is nothing really to be done as we are always already the Still Point of aware-being, but also there is much work to be done to recognize this and progressively dissolve the ego mind. Isn't that a real paradox?**

Ω: It is paradoxical to the human mind because the mind can only understand itself in the realm of doing, which seems to be our everyday experience of living in space and time. The realm of being is the Still Point, which is ever-present and unlimited, and not in space and time or bound by its rules. What this means is the recognition one has of being awareness, and not just a body-mind, does not happen in space or time but happens in the now—an instant of realization. Practically speaking, this means that for someone living in the world, and identified with their body and mind, there will appear to be much work to be done and one should absolutely do this work.

α: So, one should expect to make significant effort on the path to self-realization or enlightenment?

Ω: Yes, in fact it's ultimately a "superhuman effort," meaning the effortlessness of the Still Point accepts the seemingly intense effort of the personal thinking mind and subsumes it or brings it into itself as its source. Eventually what seemed to be "effort" is replaced by a consistent pull from the peace of the Still Point itself and the process becomes quite effortless. One remains highly vigilant to the appearance of any latent tendencies of the ego mind to reappear, but there is no strain or feeling of work.

α: A superhuman effort seems impossible, regardless of how wonderful enlightenment seems.

Ω: Here, superhuman means transcending the thinking mind—literally resting as the effortless Still Point of being that is prior to thoughts. Resting as yourself knowingly. The thinking mind can't think its way to the recognition of the Still Point, its source, nor can it understand it or describe it in any real way. When one considers their thoughts and feelings to be their actual identity, then deidentifying themselves from them seems like major work. You are changing the definition of yourself from a conceptual belief in being a body and mind that can be harmed and will die to a known understanding of being deathless, unharmable Being itself. It's a shift that is very much worth the effort.

α: *After this recognition, or shift in identity, what changes in the way we act in the world and toward others?*

Ω: Actions can look just like before, but they are more spontaneous and inclusive of what is best for everyone involved. When you see others as your very self, you no longer take actions to benefit you exclusively without thinking of others. Chores or activities that were previously seen as tedious or boring by the thinking mind may now be quite enjoyable. Whether you are cooking a delicious meal or sweeping the floor, you do so with a peaceful detached precision that comes from love.

α: *Recognition of ourself as awareness seems to be the key "starting point," but is this possible if the ego is deeply rooted and hasn't been diminished yet?*

Ω: Anyone who is sentient can recognize that they are aware. It's true that at first, they recognize awareness in relation to objects they are aware of such as sights or sounds, but the awareness is still recognized. That is why when you ask someone, "Are you aware?" they will always say yes. Even if they recognize that awareness is being aware of hearing your voice, ask them that very question. In the very early stages, the mind is so accustomed to only paying attention to the objects of awareness it can be overlooked that when the sights or sounds disappear, awareness remains aware of itself and simply available for whenever the next object of experience appears. When this is seen clearly, an important breakthrough has been reached. At this point one can rest as the Still Point of awareness alone and begin to explore its nature. Upon repeated investigation it is noticed that this awareness is always present and does not come and go like thoughts, or feelings, or even sights and sounds. At this point, when one is willing, they begin to realize that this awareness is actually what they are and not just something they possess. It is what they have called "I" their whole life. This is where self-identity starts to switch from being a body-mind to being the Still Point of awareness. This is the inception of self-realization, and if the investigation continues in earnest from this point, it will inevitably result in complete freedom. This freedom has been called many names such as happiness, salvation, enlightenment, self-realization, attainment of Buddha Nature, or Christ Consciousness, and so on.

α: *Why does it seem so hard to explore the nature of the Still Point and to come to this freedom?*

Ω: It's because most people's self-identity is so completely tied up with their thoughts that at first separating thoughts from the awareness that makes them possible seems difficult. Often times when someone is asked, "Are you aware?" and they "go" to awareness before answering yes, it is the very first time they have ever recognized that there is "something" that knows their experience. This is not taught in our schools nor in most of our religious institutions, so even though the recognition of awareness is clear, there are decades of deep "I am the body" conditioning to be dealt with. What comes with this conditioning is the belief that the thoughts and feelings one has are produced by the body (as brain), and as such, it is believed that they too are what we are. Because of this conditioning, most people must return to this recognition of the Still Point over and over again, to see our thoughts and feelings are not essential to our true nature of self-aware being.

α: *Wouldn't this process of waking up to our true nature be easier if our society taught children to recognize this early?*

Ω: Of course. The English novelist Aldous Huxley wrote a wonderful book called *Island*, which depicts a utopian society built on the knowledge that we all share the same one unlimited being. This was the last novel he published, and it stood as a counterpart to his most famous work, *Brave New World*, which depicts a very dystopian society that emerges when the ego thought system of believing we are separate beings evolves. On the island, there were Mynah birds who constantly said the words, "Attention, Here and Now," "Here and Now." This is a constant reminder to let go of continually following your thoughts off into the past or future, as most humans currently do, and return to the Still Point of awareness that knows them. This is a necessary practice to begin to shift our identity to the unlimited aware-being that we are.

THE UNNATURAL STATE
OF BOREDOM AND
IMPATIENCE

If we begin to truly examine our day-to-day experience, we will see that most of us are in a constant state of either impatience or boredom. We are always looking to the next moment, or the next experience, to come and deliver us into some sense of peace and fulfillment, but it rarely does. It rarely does because when it comes, we go right on anticipating the next moment without enjoying the peace of the only moment we are ever given, which is now. In the rare times we are not continually waiting for the promise of the next moment, we wander into the past with thought and either regret what has already occurred or fantasize about what we could have done differently. Take some time to really look at your life in this way and see how very rare the moments of true peace and relaxation are. The near constant state of unease most humans experience is usually the best-case scenario because when you add any amount of anxiety to the mix, which a huge number of people suffer from, the anticipation of the future contains a constant level of worry. With anxiety, we still continually reject the present moment in favor of a future moment, but now we also expect something bad to happen in that very future moment we pine for. This is living in bondage that has become so "normal" to most people they don't even question it or recognize its insanity.

At some points during our lives, we get something that we have been greatly desiring, such as a new job, a big house, or a romantic partner, and for a short time we are content. Instead of realizing this brief happiness is due to the cessation of the constant wanting that came from acquiring the object of our desire, we wrongly project the cause of the happiness onto the object itself. As soon as the happiness or contentment wears off, we start subtly, or not so subtly, searching for the next object to acquire to become happy again. All the while we overlook the true cause of our misery, which is the constant desire to reject the now or "what is" in favor of a better future moment. Thus, the nature of ignorant living, or "living in delusion," is living as a prisoner to thoughts. The price you pay for identifying your very self with your thoughts and feelings is unhappiness at best and misery at worst. With the rejection of your true nature as the Still Point of awareness, you willingly give up the only recognition that is happiness and peace itself.

α: *I often notice when I am waiting in line at the grocery store I am judging the person in front of me at the cashier for being too slow, or even criticizing what they are buying. What can be done?*

Ω: Recognition of this continual "edginess" or impatience is the first step to addressing it. The ego desires to be in a constant state of doing. In situations such as this, where you can't physically make the process go faster, the ego mind resorts to thinking and judging as its means of constant unfulfilled seeking. When you recognize this impatience and realize there is no action that can be taken, the situation must be accepted fully just as it is. Ask yourself, "What is aware of this impatience?" and return to the Still Point of awareness that is simply present and aware. This is your real self, and it is never impatient or judgmental. When you see clearly that it is only thinking and feeling that are compelling you to fidget and be restless, you can rest as the Still Point alone. This same practice can be employed any time you notice the mind's desire to pull you out of the now.

α: *What is the relationship of the Still Point to the now?*

Ω: They are two different ways of expressing the true nature of aware-being that is your real nature, and the real nature of all sentient beings. Remember Aldous Huxley's Mynah bird from *Island*, "Attention, here and now," "Here and now." Neither you nor anyone has ever had an experience that was not felt as happening "here" and "now." Give this deep contemplation and you will see it is always true. No matter where you seem to be in space it is felt as here, and no matter when you seem to be in time it is felt as now. This is why we can "feel" our true nature as unlimited, or infinite (always here), and ever-present, or eternal (always now). Before deeply contemplating this, when we are told we are eternal and infinite beings, the thinking mind objects saying, "I don't feel eternal or infinite," when actually that is all you ever feel. No matter where on earth you are, it is experienced as here, and no matter when you are having an experience, it is felt as now. This is why it's so important to recognize that thoughts, which constantly come and go, can never tell us about our true nature. Would you rather trust your actual felt experience, or give up all of your power to your fragile thinking mind? What is actually limited and fleeting are the thoughts you have. You, always being here and now, are there to see the thoughts rise and fall, while you, the Still Point remain.

α: *It seems easier to feel the here and now when my eyes are closed. Why is that the case?*

Ω: This is because you identify with the changing elements of experience, such as thoughts and sights, more than you do with your ever-present aware self. If you go to the beach in Hawaii, the combination of your thoughts telling you that you are in a different place, along with the sight of the beach you see, seems to override your actual felt experience of it being here and now. You have chosen to believe in things that constantly change—your thoughts and visual perceptions—as opposed to that which never changes, and is ever with you as you. When you combine this with the deeply held belief in a solid outside world made of matter, you remain a temporary, isolated being that feels it moves around in a big world that is outside and foreign to you.

α: *If you weren't lost in your thoughts and sights, wouldn't the experience of the beach be lesser?*

Ω: Absolutely not. In fact, it would be much better because nothing in the way of the beautiful images you see would be lost, but your sense of being temporary and at the mercy of an outside world would disappear.

α: *I have had anxiety much of my life and currently still take antianxiety medicine every day. I have been on this path of self-discovery for a few years and I feel like the medicine is a "crutch" at this point, but I am afraid to just stop. What should I do?*

Ω: A crutch is necessary until it is no longer needed. As you continue your exploration of the Still Point and gradually come to see it is what you are, you will notice it is peace itself. The maelstrom of anxious thoughts and feelings come only from the mind, which emanate from the Still Point, but never affect it in any way. In a sense, the Still Point is much like the eye of the hurricane—despite the furor swirling about, it remains perfectly still. As you spend more and more time resting as this unassailable peace—not following any thoughts, but simply watching the sensations in your awareness closely—you may find they lose their "bite" over time. If it becomes clear that it may be time to reduce or eliminate the medication, do so under the close care of a physician.

With any experience of fear or anxiety, it's very important to isolate the bodily sensation you feel from any thoughts that accompany it in the mind. In fact, close your eyes and sit with the sensation that is appearing in your awareness and don't allow thought to assign body locations or bodily organs as the source of the sensation. Here is where thought will try to "assign" the pure sensation a bodily cause and try to convince you that something is really wrong. Of course, with any actual pain or physical distress, seek appropriate medical attention as needed.

α: *Focus on the sensations of anxiety even if they are uncomfortable?*

Ω: Focus on them because they are uncomfortable. The only thing that gives the sensations of fear or anxiety their power is your resistance to them. Turning away from them or distracting yourself from them only makes them stronger. Likewise, letting thought intervene to tell a story about them also makes them stronger and can lead you to a sense of panic. Looking at them very closely exposes them as phantoms. The only thing the ego cannot stand is being looked at clearly because it does not actually exist. Facing the adversity of fearful or anxious sensations openly, objectively, and very closely is a wonderful way to surrender to them completely. This surrender of complete acceptance is your freedom.

α: *My thoughts seem to race almost constantly, and I am starting to see that they are not always helpful, but I have no way to seemingly stop them. What can I do?*

Ω: The recognition that your thoughts are not what you essentially are is a necessary and important step. The feeling of being the witness to your thoughts can allow thoughts to simply come and go without you attaching to them, thus eliminating the creation of more thought. The ego mind needs to be in constant motion because at its deepest level it knows its own unreality and fears stillness will expose its secret. This is why stillness and silence are the means to end the tyranny of the ego. The repeated reestablishment of the Still Point as your very being allows thought to be observed without attachment or passion. You can't fight your thoughts, or you will only strengthen them. You must simply watch them come and go while you remain as the ever-present witness. In the end, even this separation will collapse, and thought—when also seen as nothing but a movement of yourself—will lose all power over you.

α: *What do you mean by the collapse of the separation of thought and self?*

Ω: The Still Point of aware-being, your very self, is all there is to any thought you have ever had. If you were not aware of a thought, there would be no thought. When you sit in meditation as the Still Point, you will see thoughts are not always present, but you—the awareness that knows them—always remains. Thoughts arise from awareness and then dissipate back into awareness. There is thus nothing to thought but awareness itself. Thought is nothing more than a "movement" of awareness. There are never two "things" but only awareness and its movement as thoughts. Just like you can't have a movie without a screen, you can't have thoughts without the background of awareness for them to appear on.

α: *I sometimes find sitting in meditation difficult, but often when I walk in the woods I feel very calm and even lose myself in the beauty of nature. Can this be helpful?*

Ω: Yes, absolutely. Ultimately meditation is what you are as the Still Point of being, and not something you do. This is the case regardless if your eyes are open or closed or if you are sitting motionless or in movement, like walking. We often recognize nature to be complete and whole and see it needs nothing to be added or taken away. This is the experience of beauty. In the experience of beauty, there is no "you" present but rather a recognition or "merging" of awareness with the tree or the plant as itself. There is no sense of a person seeing an object, but only seeing and a recognition that you are that seeing. Much like love is a recognition of our "sameness" with people and animals, beauty is the recognition of our "sameness" with objects of nature such as trees, plants, and flowers.

α: *What about the cathartic nature of viewing art, such as paintings or other works?*

Ω: Yes, it is much the same with great art. Next time you go to the museum, walk through as though it is your very first time. Don't label the paintings or sculptures with your mind, instead just observe. You may see some works that have the power to dissolve the sense of a self, there looking at a separate object. This is the experience of beauty, and the great works of art and music created from the Still Point retain the power to "collapse" the separation between the observer and the observed.

α: *Do the artists or musicians who produce these elevated works have this understanding of their true nature as unlimited awareness?*

Ω: Some do, but many, even without the depth of this understanding, have the ability to create their work without significant filtration through the ego mind. Just as when a great athlete is "in the zone" during a game or match, the artist or musician is not present as a separate person during the creation of the work of art or the piece of music.

Art always comes from the same purity. It's the impurity of the conditioned filter system that often stains its relative perfection.

AWAKENING AND THE
LIMITS OF THE MIND

There is a great wave of awakening happening on this planet right now. A significant number of people are realizing the inability of the egos directive to deliver lasting happiness and peace. In addition, the forces of nature that represent the earth are evolving spiritually out of necessity as well. This results in a "push and pull" effect that is causing many to realize it is time to wake up to the true nature of our one unified being or risk being left behind looking for happiness in the one place it can never be found.

This "awakening" is critical to increase the "spiritual mass" on earth and to offset the deep well of unconscious action humanity has inflicted upon itself, as well as the planet and its plants and animals. One result of this drive toward transcendence is the increased interest in plant-based medicines such as ayahuasca, mushrooms, and other psychedelic compounds in the search for spiritual discovery. As there are as many nuanced paths to transcendence as there are people, no experience can be said to have no value as a learning tool as long as its limits are understood. Any experience, no matter how wonderful or awful, is still a movement of mind that happens in and is known by the Still Point of aware-being. There is no experience that alters or changes awareness—your very nature—one bit. There is no "ripening" of your true nature, nor does it expand or contract in any way. The mind can certainly "ripen," but not your true ever-present nature. The very nature of psychedelic experience "loosens" the seemingly solid reality of the waking state, and for many this can expose its dreamlike nature. Much like dreams can delight or terrify the mind while asleep, these substances can do the same while still in the waking state. Those who have done the work of repeatedly resting as the Still Point can anchor themselves "there" and ride waves of experience without letting thoughts amplify the raw experience in either direction. Much like the experience of watching a movie as an unattached observer, the ability to return and stay as the unmoving awareness you are remains invaluable. There are ultimately no shortcuts within the limits of the mind to the establishment of the Still Point of aware-being as your very self, and the necessary elimination of egoic conditioning, either before or after this recognition.

α: *Why do so many seek illumination or enlightenment through the experience of these substances?*

Ω: When you mention illumination or enlightenment, you are speaking of the "cure." There was a spiritually advanced Jesuit priest named Anthony De'Mello who said, "most people want relief but not the cure." Most people are not yet ready to discard the ego by seeing it as false, but instead are looking for relief from what ails them in the form of a short-cut. There is nothing wrong with this at all, of course, as long as it is understood that any experience anyone can ever have by nature is transient; it comes and goes. In any event, we are so thoroughly identified with our thoughts and experiences that we are convinced the answers must lie somewhere in the mind and psychedelics produce these intense experiences readily. The deep well of the subconscious mind—which we normally can't access directly—often becomes available during these experiences, and that can be perceived as frightening or blissful. Our normal state of slight ongoing resistance to everyday life can be amplified into great resistance, producing difficult experiences, or great surrender, which always is experienced as peace and joy.

α: *Is surrender the most important factor in dealing with challenging or terrifying states of mind?*

Ω: Taking your stand as the Still Point of awareness that witnesses all movement of mind, no matter how turbulent or peaceful, is akin to surrender. No matter how vivid or disturbing any experience, the Still Point, you, are untouched, and the more often you return to this, the clearer the recognition that it is your home.

α: *Many people are drawn to psychedelic experiences because they believe it will reveal their true nature in a way they can't get in everyday experience. Is this not true?*

Ω: When you ask yourself the simple question, "Am I aware?" and then say yes, you do so because you recognize you are indeed aware. This is being aware of being aware, the Still

Point that is your very self. There is nothing needed to take you to where you are already standing as the simple sense of being. In fact, any movement of thinking or imagining can only seem to take you away from yourself. It never actually does of course, but because of our deep conditioning we "follow" or attach ourselves to experience, which seems to darken the light of awareness. Everyone's mind has a different configuration, and for some, intense psychedelic experiences can seem to drive them to a "forced" recognition of that in them which never moves, but it's certainly not a shortcut. Any experience can be helpful when viewed from and as the Still Point, which can't be affected in any way.

α: *Why does it seem so hard to "separate" ourselves as the aware witness from turbulent or frightening experiences?*

Ω: This is because no experience takes place at a distance from the awareness that knows it. This is relatively easy to see with thoughts or sensations of the body because we all experience them as being within us. It's harder with visual sights or sounds because the mind, as thought, projects them as coming from a distance, or outside of ourselves. When you look at a tree in the forest, for example, the mind is telling you it's at least twenty-five or fifty meters away, as an example, the very moment it is visualized. It takes honest contemplation and experimentation to see what we perceive as the world is the same as a movie screen. This is often one of the last deep conditionings of the mind to fall in line with the true nature of reality. This is why in the early stages of this understanding we meditate with our eyes closed because it is much easier to recognize and feel that all experience happens within your awareness, and there is truly nothing outside of yourself.

α: *But even when we experience strong turbulent sensations that we feel are within us, they can still be frightening. Why is this so?*

Ω: This is because your mind tells you that they are sensations of the body, and if you remain identified as being a body, then fear or anxiety is the result. The sensations may be intense, but in and of themselves, they are neutral until thought convinces you otherwise. This is where the continual work of resting as awareness is necessary. When you see clearly that the body is experienced within you, but is not you, the sensations lose their anxious charge.

α: *What about with a chronic medical condition that causes pain—can this approach be used for pain as well?*

Ω: Yes, provided one has sought medical attention for the issue and one has done all that is reasonably possible to alleviate the pain. This is not a path of martyrdom or asceticism in any way. If appropriate treatment has been sought, regardless of the condition, the remaining discomfort must be accepted fully. Any resistance to the discomfort is the root of suffering and that is not necessary or helpful.

α: *Why does the thinking mind become so active and disruptive when I sit to meditate?*

Ω: In most people, the thinking mind is almost continually active, but because this is the "normal" state of affairs, it's not noticed. When sitting to meditate in silence, it becomes very obvious that the mind is, and has been, in near-constant movement. Thoughts come and go and "generate" other thoughts in rapid-fire succession. This is not the natural state at all but the very unnatural state of "living exclusively in the mind." When people see this, it comes as a bit of a shock to realize just what prisoners they have been to the mind. The other tactic used by the ego to avoid stillness is sleep. The ego mind is either in continuous movement or falls asleep, anything to avoid its greatest fear of being seen for what it actually is in silence.

α: *Why does the ego fear stillness and silence so much?*

Ω: The ego has no actual existence, so much like the play of light that makes up a mirage in the desert, it must remain in continuous movement to avoid being seen as illusory. If you closely examine thoughts, it's easy to see that they are not aware. Only the Still Point of awareness is aware. You are self-aware. You are aware of your thoughts, but they are not aware of themselves. When you see that thoughts or sensations and images are not aware, it begins to become clear that you have mistakenly identified yourself as these thoughts and feelings. Clearly seeing this begins to unravel the ego construct as nothing but that—a construct. After this is seen, the ego may rebel and "send" thoughts and feelings to challenge your new perspective, but it's been exposed, and its game is nearly over. At this point, returning to the Still Point and resting as its inherent awareness over and over in the midst of thoughts and feelings, as well as their absence, will expose the ego as nonexistent.

α: *How much do we need to understand the ego before it can be dissolved?*

Ω: The ego is nothing but a system of concepts and beliefs that have been "projected" onto the pristine clear Still Point since early childhood. Since it was "accepted" as your identity, it has been in the background running your life ever since. It does not need to be understood, nor does it need to be dissected or improved upon. The ego just needs to be seen clearly. With regard to the ego thought system, *A Course in Miracles* likens it to a desert and asks, "What do you do when you find yourself in a desert?" The answer is you leave. You don't try to water the arid sand or plant flowers, you simply leave. You can analyze the ego all you want, but analysis only serves to strengthen it when it just needs to be left behind. Once you know yourself as the unmovable Still Point, you will be able to see clearly the coming and going of the ego's conditioned patterns of insanity without reacting to them or following them as if they are you.

PART
II

The
Still Point

13

LIVING AS THE STILL POINT

"The voice of the river that has emptied into the ocean now laughs and sings just like God."

~ HAFIZ

If one has had a glimpse of the Still Point and recognized it as what you have been calling "I" all your life, then living as this ever-present awareness is the next logical step on the journey. Up until we have this realization, we have believed the conditioning we have received since early childhood, that we are fragile bodies and temporary minds that were born and will die. Because of this false belief, we have likely lived a contracted life as a separate self with fear of many things ruling the day. When we live with the belief and feeling of being a separate self, we are constantly trying to outrun our belief in lack by obtaining more security. When we see ourselves as separate, we naturally see others as separate, and often act toward them with fear or desire. We push them away with a million different judgements or try to get something from them to try to make us happy. We live in a state of almost continual resistance to the circumstances of our lives, or we try to grasp and hold on to fleeting moments of pleasure. Every experience we have is judged to a lesser or greater degree as being OK or not OK, and sometimes definitely not OK. This state has become so "natural" to most people, they don't even consider it anymore. Like people in a movie theatre who, not liking the film, go up to the screen and try to change it by pounding it with angry fists, as opposed to going back to the projector room to change the reel; we are fighting an impossible battle. By making the choice to live from your aware-being, you can let the movie of life play out exactly as it comes. Just like the open space of a room, you allow anything to happen within the room, even when taking action becomes necessary, only without emotional resistance or grasping. The Still Point, your very being, is completely allowing and incapable of judgement. Unlike fragile bodies, awareness doesn't come and go, nor can it be hurt in any way. This is what you are, and you will never be happy or at real peace believing you are something different. The choice between living as awareness or as a body-mind is one you must make in every moment. Living from your true nature may be easy when you are alone, or in a peaceful situation, but it is not easy when situations or people become challenging or difficult. If a person or situation is difficult and you rise up to meet it with your conditioned belief as being a separate entity, you will very likely make the situation worse. When you meet situations from your aware-being however, you come from a place of nonjudgmental love and this will ensure the best possible outcome for any challenging situation. Living as the nonjudgmental awareness that you are will also likely change your outside circumstances for the better over time as the world tends to meet us where we are standing.

Just as we need to return to the Still Point over and over during the day, we also need to be very vigilant in the way we interact with others. When we see we are being even the slightest bit defensive of our position, we are acting as the separate ego self and not defenseless awareness. We have essentially run up to the movie screen and started to hit it with our hands to try and make it change. This is the time to return to the projector room and be the projector itself, which accepts all scenes in all movies equally. The understanding of your true nature is meant to be a lived understanding. While we first rest as the truth of our being during meditation, we need to apply this discovery during our everyday lives diligently to see true transformation.

α: *I have heard a lot about mindfulness meditation. Is this a similar approach?*

Ω: Mindfulness implies giving attention to, or "watching," the movement of the mind. When attention is only given to thinking and feeling, there is a subtle or direct identification with thoughts and feelings as what we essentially are. We continue to identify ourselves with forms, in this case thought forms, that are constantly coming and going. In the direct approach to the recognition of ourselves as the Still Point, we instead relax all attention and rest as the awareness that knows these thoughts and feelings. It is here we see that thoughts and feelings arise from awareness, are known by awareness, and then dissolve back into awareness. We are that awareness and not the thoughts and feelings that casually come and go. Whenever we identify with the transient, we will believe we are transient and fear will always accompany that position. The fear may be subtle and unconscious, directing our activities from below the surface of mind, or it may be blatant, in which case we may be outwardly angry and aggressive, which is always a failed attempt to defend against this fear.

α: *Is mindfulness meditation then counterproductive?*

Ω: There is nothing done with the intention of self-realization that is counterproductive or useless. Many people who are completely identified with their thoughts and feelings may need a gradual or progressive approach at first to see the distinction between their thoughts and feelings and themselves, the Still Point of aware-being. In this day and age, many people are in fact ready to go directly to their true nature and recognize themselves as awareness. From this recognition, thoughts and feelings are still watched, but they are observed with a loving detachment. You become the pure perfect sky that simply watches the clouds, with their myriad shapes and colors, coming and going in the ever-changeless you. While this may feel like a preparation or a process, it is only gradual from the standpoint of the belief in being a person. One could say the preparation is to see that belief was always false. The moment that is clear, you will withdraw your allegiance from that false belief and remain as what you always were and always will be—vast, open, and intelligent awareness. This step is not gradual and in fact has nothing to do with time. Just like the Still Point itself, it is timeless.

α: *America is burning with racial and political protests, and the country seems to be coming apart at the seams. The protesting has been violent as well, but what is one to do?*

Ω: What will never be truly helpful is to protest injustice with violence. People may indeed be called to protest, but to be maximally effective that protest must come from a higher understanding of our unity at the deepest level of our being. We have gotten into this mess of racism and division by believing in the ego's false mantra that we are all separate people having separate individual agendas. The moment you attack and violently incite others, you are directly strengthening that false belief and repercussions are inevitable—it's karmic law. There is no denying the terrible injustice that has been happening for a long time, but treating people who are desperately calling out for love with hate and anger simply will not work. We as the human race need to definitively turn away from the insanity of the ego's belief in separation to the unity that comes from the recognition that we all share the very same being. This recognition alone has the power to turn the world into a paradise of justice and freedom, just as it was always meant to be.

α: *Should one not prioritize taking action if they are angry or upset?*

Ω: One should prioritize discovering their true nature regardless of outside circumstances. If one acts from a place of separation and division, then whatever action is taken will contain that energy, however slightly, and the action will be less than optimal. This is not to say action should not be taken, but rather that any action taken should come from the recognition that we all share the same being. There is no difference between us when we go past the differences in our thoughts and feelings to the aware presence that knows them. We are exactly the same. When we know this, our actions happen spontaneously from this place of understanding and they carry all the power of that truth. Others will see and sense this, and the truth in them will resonate with it deeply. If you want to see peace and harmony in the world, recognize the peace and harmony that you eternally are as the Still Point and you will be the blessing you want to convey to the world.

α: *These violent events happening just don't make sense. How are we supposed to understand the greater reason for such cruelty?*

Ω: Any person's individual mind can't possibly see all of the factors that led to the occurrence of any event or series of events that takes place in the world. Just as we are all completely interconnected, so too are the seemingly random events that take place on the screen of the world. This is why changing the world must be secondary to changing your mind *about* the world. Fighting or judging any event that happens in the world or any circumstance that happens to you is a losing battle. Giving up the battle and accepting all circumstances is the only way to peace and happiness. This does not mean we condone rude or violent behavior at all but rather that we accept "what is" and act, when necessary, from our true nature as the Still Point, which is love itself.

α: *But some events are harder to accept than others, right?*

Ω: There remains judgement in that approach and it is not true acceptance. If what you are is completely untouchable awareness, then no matter how intense events or circumstances seem to be, they can't hurt you in any way. As *A Course in Miracles* says, "There is no order of difficulty in miracles. One is not "harder" or "bigger" than another. They are all the same. All expressions of love are maximal." Here the miracle refers to forgiveness, which can also be viewed as total acceptance. The Still Point, your true nature, is as completely accepting as the space of a room in which events occur. You can easily see that regardless of what events happen in the room, it is completely accepted by the space. One event is not "harder" to accept then another, regardless of how unconscious it seems to be. Again, this never means we condone unconscious behavior on the part of others, but if we reply, or act, from a place of judgement, we are unwittingly reinforcing the belief in separation that is characteristic of the ego belief system.

α: *During these last months in relative isolation due to the pandemic, I've realized I need far less than I ever previously believed was required. Fewer material things in general, and less frequent social interaction. But yet I am even happier. Doesn't this correspond to a deeper understanding of ourselves as the Still Point of awareness?*

Ω: The Still Point is what you are, what we all are at our deepest core of being. It is whole and complete by its nature. It has never come or gone but remains as the sense of "I" you have had at all times in your life. It cannot die or be affected in any way. While your outside circumstances have changed these last months, you have begun to realize that what you truly are is utterly unaffected by any of those changes and that recognition carries the seed of liberation. This self-discovery frees you from the mistaken reliance on outside circumstances for your peace and happiness. When you realize yourself as this complete ground of being, you carry its innate peace with you wherever you seem to go and whatever you seem to do in the world.

α: *Life has certainly been different for all of us this last year, and certainly very chaotic at times. Regardless, many people I know have found some relief in meditating and looking within. Is this a bit of a blessing in disguise?*

Ω: Life itself is a great spiritual teacher. It will present whatever circumstances you need in order for you to exercise your ever-present choice of acceptance or resistance. If you take an attitude of gratitude for challenging situations, you will see a quantum acceleration of peace and joy regardless of the circumstances at hand. This not only applies to "outside" circumstances but to our minds as well. If at the moment feelings of fear or anxiety arise and you choose to face them directly, you have the opportunity to see what these feelings are truly made of—nothing but the Still Point in motion. It is the pushing away of difficult feelings that gives them their power over you. Even slight resistance or a "secret" wish to abolish these feelings will ensure they not only continue, but also get stronger. This resistance is the suffering itself. The end of resistance is the end of suffering, but it must be a total surrender to whatever is being resisted: a feeling, a life situation, or anything else. We are so accustomed and programmed to "move away" from uncomfortable feelings by taking action that we perpetually reinforce their "otherness," and this ensures their survival. Even if it is just for a short time before you distract yourself, turn toward the feeling or sensation and face it completely. This is where you will need to disengage from any thinking about the situation and just face the raw feeling itself. If this is done with complete acceptance, you will inevitably see that the feeling or sensation is nothing but your aware-being vibrating within itself alone. This recognition is the relief you seek.

α: *Is there a way to accelerate the process of self-discovery or is making more effort ultimately counterproductive?*

Ω: When what you are calling the "process of self-discovery" is undertaken with sincere love for truth, the concept of "effort" eventually collapses. It is only the ego mind that protests self-discovery and calls it effort. When one has a burning love for truth, it is an effortless courtship. There is no doubt that at first it may feel like effort from the ego's perspective, and that should be endured until greener pastures prevail. The paradox of "effortless effort" is always at play when what you seek is the timeless being that you already are. Regardless, you should turn your attention to self-discovery as often as it is truly enjoyable. You will find much greater "progress" is made when you feel compelled to meditate and contemplate the Still Point when you love doing so freely, and not out of timed obligation.

α: *In living as the Still Point, do we see and feel that others are one with us, or the same as us?*

Ω: When you have recognized that your actual felt experience is awareness aware of itself and you rest as this very awareness in meditation, you come to see it is whole and has no parts or boundaries. This aware-being that you are is not two and is thus the only being there that is shared by all sentient beings, both humans and animals alike. This is the experience of love itself and it is naturally extended to "others" when you stop thinking and feeling that you are separate. In the early stages, when you intellectually understand that we all share the same being, you will intellectually see others as the same as you. Later, when you know and feel that we share the same being, you will powerfully feel this love with all creatures. This does not mean you will like or want to spend time with everyone because compatibility on that level is much more driven by the personality, which of course is different for everyone.

α: *When one is enlightened or knows their true nature, doesn't their personality diminish or disappear?*

Ω: No, not at all. The identification one had as being the personality as well as the body goes, but the personality does not. In fact, the personality may blossom in many ways once the mind is freed from the incorrect association with thinking and feeling. If the personality seems to change, it is likely just a return to what was its original or inherent state before the ego sent one down the endless path of trying to fulfill itself. A person who was very outgoing and talkative as a learned egoic behavior to try and "get ahead" in the world may become quieter and more reflective upon dis-covering they are whole and complete and need do nothing to enhance themselves. Of course, it could be the other way around or any other combination, but a unique personality certainly remains.

TAKING
RESPONSIBILITY FOR
YOUR HAPPINESS

Living as the Still Point means taking radical responsibility for your state of mind in all circumstances. When you begin to see that the aware-being you are is the same aware-being shared by all, there can be no "others" who determine your happiness. This recognition may at first be a bit overwhelming to the concept of the ego mind you had previously believed yourself to be. The desire to project blame on others, the world, or past events is a universal trait of the egoic mind. As you begin to see the ego as a nonexistent belief, you begin to take true responsibility for your state of being in every moment. Thoughts will certainly arise that follow the old conditioning of blaming others during difficult situations, but this is the time to see them for what they are and drop them immediately. Once you act on one of these old thought habits, you will likely immediately see the negative effect they have on others and on the situation in general. Defending a point of view will almost always invite reprisals from others who still believe they are separate ego selves. On the other hand, coming from a place of defenselessness will, in most instances, cause others to do the same, or at the very least, soften their stance. When you begin to consistently interact with others in a defenseless way, the quality of the interactions, and the relationship in general, begins to improve. Over time, the old conditioned thoughts imploring you to defend a point of view or blame others stops arising with such frequency because you already know they will not be helpful. This is an important step, especially in your close and intimate relationships. When you consistently interact in an open, defenseless way, your spouse or partner will often begin to do the same. Taking responsibility for yourself is a powerful lesson to those around you who may not yet see the value in shedding old defensive habits.

Over time, one may begin to view their interactions with friends differently as well. Many times, when "friends" gather it is primarily to validate each other's points of view with various forms of "people-pleasing." In many groups when someone blames their spouse or partner (who is usually not present) for something that has occurred, the expectation is that the others will rush in to validate their hurt feelings. This is both unhelpful and unloving, despite what they may think. It's very possible that certain friendships will fall away naturally due to your new understanding, and that is perfectly fine. In time, you will attract people who share the recognition that we must take responsibility for our own peace and happiness. This never means we condone unconscious behavior perpetrated on us or others, but taking someone's side only because "that's what friends do" becomes unacceptable. Most people have a greater capacity to deal with the truth than they are given credit for by society, and you are never doing anyone a favor by validating false beliefs. When you act and behave as the completely accepting Still Point, you encourage others to do the same and that is the greatest contribution to their happiness you can ever give.

α: *Sometimes I can tell my friend is disappointed I am not taking her side or supporting her when she has arguments with her husband, but it seems they are both being defensive. What is the best approach?*

Ω: Validating anyone's egoic perspective is not supporting them at all but rather reinforcing their sense of separation, which ultimately is reinforcing their misery. It's enough that you see this and act accordingly in all situations. There can be no harmony until at least one member of the warring party drops their egoic need to defend themselves and be right. Friendship is not true friendship if you don't point this out in a loving way. After all, in encouraging a friend to give up the need to be right, you are simply encouraging them to be what they truly are as the Still Point, which has no personal point of view that must be enforced.

α: *Is it helpful to seek the company of friends who share the same interest in self-realization?*

Ω: You alone are responsible for your state of presence in all situations. Sincere dedication to spiritual growth will usually attract like-minded people to you without the need to plan it in a certain way. The people who are in your life now already present perfect learning opportunities regardless of their specific beliefs. It's a common trap to think we need to swap out partners or friends to give us a better chance at awakening.

There is a resistance in that to what is in the now, and that is the seed of suffering itself. Treating everyone in an open, loving, and nonjudgmental way is the only real way to ensure the best relationships possible. In this way, some friends who are not ready to abandon the need for egoic validation will naturally fall away from you; others will just as surely appear.

α: *My family is traditionally religious but not happy at all. What is the best way to approach them with this understanding in the hope they will begin to look within themselves for peace?*

Ω: The only way is to live this understanding so they can see your "real-life" example. In this way, your peace and happiness may be a beacon that causes them to ask you specifically what has changed with you. In that case you can tell them directly how you came to this new understanding. It's very often not helpful, or even counterproductive, to try and impose this approach to self-understanding on them. If they are involved in a traditional religion with duality as its base, they may still be receiving some solace from that belief system, and that should be respected. Challenging their belief system when they are not ready can be frightening to them and that is never helpful. Let your loving actions and behavior stir their curiosity so that a true question can be formulated by them to you and then answered appropriately.

α: *My wife and I have been on the direct path for a few years after coming from a Buddhist background. Although much better, we still have occasional arguments and don't seem to "reconnect" for a day or two after. Is there something we can do to shorten this time?*

Ω: Recognize that you have wandered away from the Still Point and taken on the defense of an egoic separate self. Sitting in meditation as this awareness should quickly reestablish this fact. This is the value of having glimpsed or recognized this truth already. Of course, when this is reestablished, you will clearly see that you were acting on behalf of the separate person you once believed you were. Lovingly apologize for having acted on behalf of the ego and move forward as the Still Point, remaining only in the now. There is no need to dissect past disagreements but only to see that you had temporarily "forgotten yourself." If you are waiting for an apology from your partner first, or still feel some anger, you have not yet fully returned to taking your stand as awareness and not the ego. It's very important to see this because any further interaction from this perspective will only create more conflict.

α: *Yes, but I feel we should both apologize to be able to move forward together. Is this not the case?*

Ω: Any belief in the need for a "quid pro quo" comes only from the ego and never awareness. As hard as that may be to see in the moment, you can only control your own reactions by choosing to live as the Still Point. The very best chance you have of affecting your partners choice is to return and live as this openness and peace that never judges and is loving by nature. This is a contagious state of being and others are deeply affected by its presence in a positive way.

THE ABSOLUTE NEED TO SEE THE EGO SELF AS FALSE

When pure awareness seems to contract into a human mind, it also associates itself with a form that is experienced as the body. Just like a telescope lens needs to focus to see any particular image, pure awareness, our true self, needs to do the same for us to experience the world from a particular point of view. This experience of "seeing through our own eyes," combined with deep conditioning by society and an amassed collection of judgements, is what seems to create the egoic or separate self that most people think and feel themselves to be. In a sense, this cycle of mind associating with a "body" repeats itself every night when we enter the dream state. In dreams, we project a new body into the dream world and seem to see it from that perspective, just as we do in the waking state. This "dream body" seems to create another "dream separate self" that is experienced just like our physical body when "awake." Finally, when the dream dissolves, the Still Point of awareness "relaxes" like the telescope lens and remains blissfully aware of only itself. This is why everyone loves deep sleep.

When we believe we are a separate self, our thoughts often reflect that belief and they arise in continuous judgement of experience. Some experiences are judged as good and others bad. From this faulty perspective, we then seek or desire the "good" experiences and resist the "bad" ones. This was Shakespeare's point in *Hamlet* when he said, "for there is nothing either good or bad, but thinking makes it so." This perspective keeps us in the circle of pleasure and pain—forever desiring the pleasure and resisting the pain.

This is what the existentialist philosophers concluded, and the summation of their philosophy can essentially be summarized as "existence is hell." "Existence" here meaning to "stand apart" as a separate human personality, or in other words to believe you are the separate ego self. Without understanding and feeling that one is the Still Point of aware-being, the belief in being the ego is indeed often absurd and hellish.

In essence, the ego or separate self is nothing but the false belief that we are the "agency" of awareness that allows this human experience to appear as it does. The separate self is literally just a point of view. The problem arises only when we identify with this ego as our very self and believe its constant seeking and resisting are necessary. When we do this, we overlook the only reality the ego has, which is awareness itself. This awareness, the Still Point, seeks and resists nothing. It's no wonder why most people are in such states of discontentment or outright misery because they continually act in such opposition to the open acceptance of their true nature. The only solution to this is to see the ego as being completely made up, simply by believing in it. You can study or try to improve the ego all you want, but in the end that will never grant one peace and happiness. The Still Point is peace and happiness itself and any remaining tendrils of belief in the ego being what you are will only obscure this truth and keep one in misery.

α: *If I recognize the Still Point as what I am, my very being, won't that eliminate the ego?*

Ω: When you see and accept that you are awareness, you will also begin to see much more clearly the patterns of conditioned thought and behavior that constitute what we are calling ego, or the separate self. Even when you have initially given up the full belief in being the ego or separate self, the patterns of conditioning are so very deeply embedded that they will continue to emerge for some time. For example, when the body gets an illness, the feeling of being unwell often serves to "contract" us back into body identification, which is often reflected in us being short or cranky to those around us. During these times you may need to ask, "What is experiencing these symptoms?" over and over again to return you to your aware-being, which remains pristinely unaffected. As one practices this, the discernment you have improves to the point where even when not feeling well, the awareness that knows these feelings and sensations is unmistakable. Returning to and living from the Still Point will also ensure the most rapid return to health possible in any situation.

α: *You mentioned the contraction of pure awareness into the body-mind or separate self as necessary to see and interact with the world as we do, but why did this separation happen in the first place?*

Ω: Inherent in that question is the very belief that a "separation" did, in fact, happen. Any answer given would seem to validate that belief. In fact, no separation has or could ever happen. It is your experience that you have always been aware at all times and under all circumstances. In the waking state, you are aware of your experiences as you are aware of the dreams in the dream state. In deep sleep awareness remains only aware of itself. Pure awareness, the ground of being, is whole and complete eternally, and any belief in being separate, or separation itself, is just that—a false belief.

α: *What about unconscious states such as being under general anesthesia or passing out?*

Ω: They are the very same as deep sleep. Just as no one dislikes or fears deep sleep, no one awakes from anesthesia with any complaints about the "experience" itself. You may recall the fear or worry about the operation, or the pain or nausea felt right after waking, but the actual state of being under general anesthesia is peace itself.

α: *I have been on a non-dual path for years and lately have seen the ego as false. Instead of feeling good, I feel more depressed than ever, even hopeless at times. The things I used to enjoy just don't bring pleasure anymore. Is there anything to do here that can help?*

Ω: Winston Churchill gave good advice when he said, "If you're going through hell, keep going." This is a common and very difficult part of the seeming path you are on. It has been described by many Christian mystics, such as St. John of the Cross, as "The Dark Night of the Soul." This of course has variations but is generally a time when the ego or separate self that one believed themselves to be for decades has been seen to be just a false belief. When this happens, often the pleasures the ego thrived upon lose their luster and experience can seem completely bland for a time, leading to feelings of depression or hopelessness. In this case, while one has recognized the ego as false and the Still Point of awareness as their actual self, they have not yet seen clearly the nature of awareness as peace and happiness itself. This is a time where great determination is needed. Determination to continually return to the Still Point of aware-being that knows the feelings of depression. It is often in these times when experience feels dark and intense that the Still Point reveals its unlimited and ever-present luminosity. In any event, this "stage" is real progress, and though it may feel like a "no-man's-land," the fertile fields of peace and joy that await are well worth the price of admission.

α: *You mention the ego is just a belief, but it seems more complex than that. Aren't beliefs just transient, coming and going too?*

Ω: Saying "the ego seems to be more complex than just a belief" is nothing more than itself a belief. Most people have no idea just how limiting their beliefs are and what a price they pay for maintaining them. A belief comes from nothing but thoughts that have been reinforced over and over until they attain the "status" of becoming a belief. Unfortunately, at this point, one stops investigating the original question, sometimes for a lifetime. Add to that the fact that most of those initial thoughts that became beliefs were just placed into you from the outside, by parents or society, and you realize they were never even yours to begin with. For example, a child is told by their parents that they are such and such a religion and God is a being that looks like a human who lives in a place at an infinite distance away called Heaven. The child accepts this as a belief without any experience of this being true at all. Human history is rife with murder and war over nothing but unverified beliefs. This is why the point of "turning around" to look within for truth can also be described as the willingness to question all of one's beliefs in the search for happiness or salvation.

16

THE HORIZONTAL
AND VERTICAL ASPECT
OF LIFE

Much like an *x* and *y* graph, life has both a horizontal and vertical dimension in play at all times. The horizontal aspect can be seen as the physical body and mind, or the person, moving along a line of what seems to be time. Along this horizontal line is our "physicality" as well as our thinking minds with their specific knowledge-based intelligence. We are relatively limited on the horizontal plane by genetics and such, but we still can change "ourselves" here through things like physical exercise and formal and informal education. One can become a bit faster or stronger physically and increase their relational knowledge by studying various disciplines such as science, art, language, and philosophy. Regardless of how much "work" we do, we move or evolve along this horizontal spectrum relatively little in the grand scheme. On the other hand, the *y* axis, or vertical aspect of life, is the spiritual aspect and here everyone has unlimited ability to move either up or down at all times and under all circumstances. (It must be noted that at a certain point of spiritual development up the vertical dimension the glimpse of truth seen cannot be undone.) At the "bottom" of the vertical dimension is a complete belief and feeling that one is nothing but the isolated ego self at the mercy of others and the cruel world. Most people are unfortunately still near the bottom of this dimension, but that is changing rapidly on this planet now. Here, at the lowest levels, we see this expressed as anything from physical violence, including war and murder, to certain states of psychosis and other "mental" illnesses. As one moves up the vertical aspect, one is progressively divested of their sense of separation and eventually recognizes themselves, and everyone else, to be the Still Point of being. One unified aware-being that vibrates within itself to seems to create all the aspects of the universal reality we experience every day. There is no one, regardless of IQ or physical stature, who does not have the same potential for complete self-realization. In fact, at the "top" of the vertical dimension is the realization that there are in reality no "others," just clusters of the one awareness that have contracted and are now appearing as physical bodies in the dreamlike play of the waking state. Once this recognition is clearly seen, the bonds of separation fall away and liberation appears as peace and happiness that no longer depend on outside circumstances.

α: *Does reading or studying a spiritual text or discipline move one slightly up the vertical plane?*

Ω: Moving up the vertical aspect requires at least a "softening" of the belief that one is a separate ego self. Amassing any knowledge, even about a spiritual system, adds only to one's horizontal development unless it moves beyond an intellectual understanding to a known, felt understanding of our true nature. This is the problem with many modern religious institutions in that they have completely forgotten that the vertical dimension is the only "place" where salvation or enlightenment can be found.

α: *Many "realized" teachers seem to be intelligent, so it surely must play some role?*

Ω: The level of worldly, relational intelligence one has does not affect one's ability to recognize their true nature as the Still Point of aware-being in any way. Worldly intelligence may affect how this understanding, once realized, is expressed in language, but it does not affect the realization of the understanding at all. There have been many realized teachers who exude deep innate intelligence despite having relatively limited formal education. The great Indian sage Nisargadatta Maharaj had a very limited formal education yet expressed this understanding in a simple yet deeply profound way.

α: *If there is "nothing" but one unified awareness that we all are, doesn't the horizontal all happen within the vertical anyway?*

Ω: Yes, the knowing of any physical or mental experience is necessary to actually have the experience. If you remove the knowing, which is awareness, no experience would ever be had. All analogies used—whether the horizontal and vertical dimension, or the sky and the clouds, the actor and the character, and so on—are just a means of trying to illustrate that which ultimately can't even be spoken of. Language itself implies duality, and if one were to truly teach from the perspective of the Still Point, silence would be necessary. As *A Course in Miracles* says, "Words are but symbols of symbols twice removed from reality."

α: *What do you mean by saying words are twice removed from reality?*

Ω: The word sugar is not sweet. The taste may be sweet, which is once removed from the awareness that knows it, so using a word to describe this is thus twice removed from reality.

α: *In meditating daily and working to eliminate the ego, I am beginning to see just how many minor things can cause me to contract into a separate self that needs defending. It seems like when I eliminate one egoic attachment, there are so many others that then emerge. Is there any way to hasten the process?*

Ω: Working or fighting to eliminate the ego will only strengthen it. The ego is a belief and has no reality other than what you give it. It's true that as you begin to establish yourself as the Still Point, you will see just how often you react on behalf of the egoic or separate self, though you will never find this phantom self upon deep investigation. Ask yourself, "On whose behalf am I reacting?" and look within for this entity that has been running your life. All you will find is the Still Point, your aware-being, which resists or reacts to nothing. The only way to "hasten" the process of dropping egoic patterns is to see, with more and more clarity, that there is no ego to be found. One can't eliminate egoic attachments one-by-one, but only see its complete nonexistence.

BE A TRUE STUDENT
OF PEACE AND
HAPPINESS

In his book *The Heart of the Enlightened*, Anthony de Mello retells a story that helps illustrate how rare true seekers are:

> When the King visited the monasteries of the great
> Zen master Lin Chi, he was astonished to learn that
> there were more than ten thousand monks living there
> with him. Wanting to know the exact number of the
> monks, the King asked, "How many disciples do you
> have?" Lin Chi replied, "Four or five at the very most."

The Zen master is pointing out that while many take on the role of students, true disciples who are willing to establish themselves as the Still Point and give up their egoic conditioning are very rare. Without having a true love of truth and desire for lasting peace and happiness, the goal will remain elusive for many. It is only after recognizing that our true nature, the sense of being "I," is awareness and not the "story" you and society have made up for you, that one can begin to truly walk the pathless path to understanding. For all of the benefits the modern world has provided in terms of increasing exposure to many teachings, the risk of one coming across watered-down or patently misleading approaches is heightened. If one has resonated with the direct approach to self-realization discussed here, then radically commit to recognizing yourself as the Still Point of aware-being, and then to seeing clearly that it is, meaning you are, always present, never coming and going, and that you are whole and complete already and always. Any teacher or teaching that is uncompromisingly direct will continually "turn one back" to the immediacy of one's true nature of aware presence. Every desire one has ultimately comes from the Still Point. It is the very pull of happiness itself. Direct teachings that are honest to the lineage understand that and return the student to that most intimate "sense" of being aware that is ultimately the true teacher itself. Once we have recognized the Still Point as what we are, we only need to relax our attention into it and rest as the completely open and allowing presence over and over again, to taste the peace and happiness that are its very nature.

Words are ultimately not important and must become secondary to your felt experience of being awareness itself. We have used many words to point to this felt experience. The Still Point, Awareness, I, Being, Presence, the Still Point of aware-being, Consciousness, to name just a few, are all words used here to approach, or point to, exactly the same thing, which is the simple nonobjective experience of being aware.

α: *I have been taking the direct approach for a few years now, but I admit I get bored and spend time with other teachings out of frustration. Why does this frustration arise?*

Ω: Boredom and frustration are resistance mechanisms of the ego self. In fact, the ego is nothing but the activity of seeking and resisting. Until the ego is seen as false, the mind will willingly entertain thoughts that compel one to move away from resting as awareness and to reengaging the mind in its own search for truth and happiness. Truth can never be realized at the level of the thinking mind. The ego thought system must remain in continual movement or risk being seen and exposed as unreal. This is why, if you have undertaken a direct approach, seeing it through makes sense.

α: *What are some of the hallmarks of a true student of spirituality, or even just one looking to be truly happy, and why are they so rare?*

Ω: Absolute love of truth springs from the clear recognition that happiness can't be found in external objects of any kind, including relationships and states of mind. It only arises when one has had enough of suffering. This is not only the "big" suffering—such as states of depression or anxiety, continual conflicts in relationships and the like—but also very subtle suffering that is an internal feeling of restlessness or boredom in seemingly normal situations. Once one has recognized that they have sacrificed their happiness by only searching for it externally in the world, they fully turn within and become a true student.

α: *I have heard that enlightenment is not possible to achieve but it is an accident of God or nature. Is this true?*

Ω: What you call enlightenment is simply knowing your own being and its ever-present and unlimited nature. This realization can't be made or understood by the thinking mind, so in that sense no "person" achieves this understanding. This is an understanding that transcends the belief in being a limited person altogether. This is what the Zen master Suzuki Roshi meant when he said, "Enlightenment is an accident and spiritual practice makes us accident prone."

α: *If lasting happiness can't be found in any external experiences, can we enjoy experience once we have come to understand our true nature?*

Ω: You may truly enjoy experience for the first time ever! The difference is that now any activity you undertake flows from happiness and not toward happiness. The "seeking" aspect is now removed from any experience one has and experience is allowed to be exactly as it is.

α: *There seems to be repetitive simplicity in returning to or resting as the Still Point. Is there a more advanced teaching?*

Ω: Resting or abiding as the Still Point, while knowing it as your true nature, is the highest teaching. The highest meditation is to simply be aware of being aware. The thinking mind will vacillate between telling you this is "simple" or "impossible" because its goal is to keep moving at all costs. It "knows" it can only sustain its power over you by remaining in continual movement. This is why your true power is resting as the

Still Point and letting thoughts come and go exactly as they please, without following them or attaching yourself to them in any way.

α: *If the thinking mind is the biggest obstacle to realization, how do we address the subconscious or unconscious mind?*

Ω: The thinking mind in and of itself is not a problem. Identifying yourself with thoughts and feelings is a problem. Certain beliefs that reside in the subconscious mind show themselves in the way of feelings. These can be feelings of anxiety, unease, or outright fear. These "feelings" must be isolated from any conscious thought and will then be revealed as nothing but neutral sensations floating within the field of awareness. Facing these feelings directly is the way to address the deep subconscious mind that is normally inaccessible. Once the feelings that arise from subconscious beliefs are seen to be nothing but neutral sensations, and thus accepted completely, the unconscious beliefs that caused them begin to dissipate as well.

The thinking mind is much like the moth that desperately seeks the flame of the Still Point. It doesn't know that it must dissolve into the flame to be transformed from a dictator of chaos into a servant of truth.

18

LEAVING THE DREAM
THOUGHT CREATES

Most people do not realize they are living in a false dreamlike world created by their thoughts. When the seventeenth century philosopher René Descartes said, "I think therefore I am," he was astutely stating what most of humanity still believes to this day—that we are our thoughts. Despite the fact that all thoughts are fleeting, lasting seconds at most, very few investigate that which remains in between, as well as before and after thought. If one closes their eyes and observes thought, there is an unmistakable sense of being that remains after one thought has ceased and before another begins. This is the Still Point. It is not only present between thoughts but rather it is ever-present. This is the "reality" that gives us the sense "I am." This sense that "I am" is the highest spiritual pointer leading directly to our true nature. Instead of giving this deep, ever-present mystery attention, we give almost all of our attention to the virtual world that our incessant thinking creates in nearly every moment. I say "creates," but "miscreates" would be a better word because the virtual world created by the thinking mind is vastly inferior to the actual world of raw, nonjudgmental experience. When we believe that thinking is part of who we are, along with our feelings and the physical body, the world we seem to live in is mostly lived in our heads, created by the continual stream of thinking that labels and judges everything. When we meet a friend over a casual drink, for example, we bring into the encounter a huge number of past associations and judgements about that person that completely cloud the "reality" of the experience with the thinking mind. We are not meeting that person, really—our thoughts and beliefs about who we are is meeting who we think and believe that person to be. This is why most conversations follow along conditioned patterns of thinking that we have already established, and are far from fresh, open, and novel. When you see this, you realize this is the same with almost every experience we have. Most people's experience is filtered exclusively through the thinking mind, and this drastically limits the experience itself. This is not to state that thoughts and memories are not necessary for the human experience, but we have long ago surrendered the purity and joy of raw experience to the limits and judgements of the thinking mind.

The solution to this is to see clearly that we are not our thoughts, nor is anyone else for that matter. We can't possibly manage the "thinking problem" with behavioral control but only come to see that we actually "are" the aware presence that underlies all thought and remains in the absence of thought as well. This recognition of who we really are prior to thinking initially creates a little space between the incessant stream of thinking we are normally lost in. When this "space" is created, we begin to see just how much of a slave we have been to thinking. We recognize that we have been living in a world "built" by layer upon layer of thought that feeds upon itself. This is the dreamlike state of the thinking mind and it is often not a great dream. It is a dream of judgment, likes and dislikes, and a continual movement away from the peace and joy of the now. Returning again and again to the simple experience of awareness and letting thoughts come and go without attachment allows us the recognition that we have never been our thoughts, and we do not need to remain in their bondage. Gradually the thinking process slows, and the peace and happiness of our true nature begins to emerge. In time, the nature of thoughts, when they do arise, change to reflect this recognition of our true nature, and thought becomes a helpful servant to the Still Point of ever-present being instead of the master that once ruled you mercilessly.

α: *My thoughts tend to race when I meditate. Is there a way for me to think better thoughts as I investigate the Still Point?*

Ω: The belief that you produce your thoughts is equivalent to believing that you are your thoughts—that they are your identity. If you examine this very closely, you will find no one creating or producing thoughts. After a thought arises you may have another thought arise that tells you, "That was my thought," but it too simply arose from the ground of your being. When one identifies with the ego self, the thoughts that arise are usually conditioned patterns of reactivity to the circumstances around you or previous lines of thinking. The only way to break these patterns is to see you are not your thoughts, but the Still Point from which they arise and dissolve back into.

α: *What do you mean when you say our world is built by layers of thought?*

Ω: When you look at a picture on a flat TV screen, you are seeing nothing but shapes and colors until thought conceptualizes and names individual objects. Each "object" has many associations you have come to give it over time, whether it's a dog or a telephone, for example. Thinking also builds many relationships between these objects and a world is born, despite the fact that you are looking at a single, unified screen. This is the same when viewing the world. You conceptualize objects, but those objects have only the meaning that you have given them from your previous conditioning. This is what Krishnamurti meant when he said, "The day you teach the child the name of the bird, the child will never see that bird again."

α: *It seems that so many spiritual traditions point out thinking, or the thinking mind, as being such a problem. If thinking causes suffering, why is it so central to the human condition?*

Ω: Thinking does not cause suffering, but believing that you think and that you are your thoughts is the very root of suffering itself. Thoughts come and go continually, and this is not hard for anyone to see, but you never witness yourself coming and going. This belief that you are a separate, limited self is the cause of all suffering. When you do not see that you are the Still Point that precedes all thought and remain when thought dissipates, you think you are cut off from your source. Thinking itself, when thoughts are required or are creatively coming from the unified mind, are a necessary and useful aspect of life.

α: *I'm having difficulty understanding how conditioned thoughts create the world as we see it.*

Ω: Let's say you are lying in the grass on a warm summer day with your eyes closed. When you open your eyes, visual perception arises and you see a single white object inside a vast blue background. This experience does not take place at any distance from you, however thought immediately arises, along with the visual perception, and tells you it is a single cloud in the blue sky many thousands of feet away. Your conditioned thinking has taken a visual perception that "happens" inside you and projects it "out," labeling individual objects at a great distance from you. It makes you feel like there is a you inside, and a world outside, that is separate and independent from you. Just like when you look at a flat-screen TV, your thinking mind projects depth and distance where there are none. This is the very same thing that happens when we look at the world along with thought.

α: *So then seeing itself is not an issue, but the issue is the way the mind interprets what we see?*

Ω: Yes, the illusion is not what we are seeing but rather how the mind conceptualizes it into a world "out there," which seems to mean there is an "us" in here. Because of this, most people feel separate and at the mercy of the outside world. In reality, any experience anyone has ever had, whether a sight or sound, takes place inside the Still Point of our aware-being. Most of us already feel like thoughts, tastes, smells, and sensations happen inside of us, but sights and sounds are projected out and we think they happen at a distance from ourselves. These thoughts are so deeply engrained in us that it takes deep and committed investigation to see that all experience happens inside of awareness or knowing, which is our shared being.

α: *Are there other helpful ways to see that any experience we have takes place inside of us and not "out there"?*

Ω: Can you have any experience at all without "knowing" it? Take a random sight you are having of a tree and ask what would there be if you removed the knowing aspect of this experience. There would be no sight at all. This is the same for sounds, tastes, even thoughts. You can reduce any experience you have ever had to the knowing aspect of it, or it would never have been an experience in the first place. This knowing is the self-aware Still Point. Your very being is the self-aware Still Point, and it is the only "thing" that has awareness as an inherent property of itself. Thus, without the self-aware Still Point, there could be no experience at all. This is the gateway to the understanding that any experience is nothing but the Still Point vibrating within itself. It is only thought that labels and classifies experience to give name and form to these vibrations, thus "creating" the world.

> *"And as imagination bodies forth*
> *the forms of things unknown, the poet's pen*
> *turns them to shapes and gives to airy nothing*
> *a local habitation and a name."*
>
> ~ WILLIAM SHAKESPEARE,
> *A MIDSUMMER NIGHT'S DREAM*

19

THE ILLUSION OF CONTROL

Until you recognize that aspect of yourself that can never be taken away, you will never find true happiness. For most people, moments of happiness or joy are short lived and subject to outside circumstances conforming to some standard their ego has decided to set. This short-lived joy comes when some desired object has been attained and remains as long as desire drops away. The moment desire returns, joy slowly morphs back into unhappiness as seeking returns. The most unfortunate part of this short-lived joy is that it reinforces the false belief that it was the acquisition of the wanted object or relationship that brought the joy in the first place. This is never true as it is actually the cessation of the seeking or desire for the object that was the cause. Armed with this frivolous reinforcement, the ego, unhappy again, doubles down on its effort in the search for the next object or relationship to end its suffering. Most people can't see that suffering is caused by the seeking itself. How many people over the course of the centuries have attained fame, wealth, and relationships galore, only to take their own life in some exquisite mansion? To add to this confusion, if you grew up in the Western world at least, you have been indoctrinated into a society of rampant consumerism since birth. You have likely been subject to an almost constant barrage of messages teaching you that happiness lies in "having more." In fact, the ego's dictum of "seek but do not find" almost perfectly describes the message of Western society over the last few hundred years.

As the world has increasingly become a "global village," many traditional Eastern cultures have been "infected" with this false ideal as well. One can have money, a nice home, cars, or any other object within reason, as long as they don't "have" you. This is not a subtle difference at all, but actually a very deep and profound difference. If the possession of any object, beyond those needed to live safely and comfortably, is believed to be needed for happiness, there remains an unhealthy attachment at play. Again, nice things can be enjoyed tremendously if one has truly seen that lasting happiness can only come from the knowing of our own indestructible being. Paraphrasing Jesus in the Gospel of Matthew, "Seek first the Kingdom of Heaven and the rest will be given you." Here, seeking the Kingdom of Heaven means seeking the knowing of your own being as the unlimited and always present Still Point. This knowing is lasting happiness and peace itself.

In their search for happiness, most people are in a near-constant battle to control as much around them as possible. This is primarily related to their personal "story" and the image of themselves they have created. The problem is you can't control your way to happiness. In fact, if one were to look closely, we are actually in very little control of many things, including the inherent functioning of our physical bodies. Our hearts beat by themselves and we couldn't stop breathing for long, even if we wanted to. The astronomical number of complex bio-chemical reactions that occur within our bodies that are necessary for life every day are not under our conscious control at all. When you also see clearly that we are not the "thinkers" of our thoughts, but rather they simply arise from and fall back into the Still Point, you begin to see the absolute folly of continuing this approach of maniacally trying to control our way to happiness. In fact, this desire to control every-thing is what is actively keeping us in misery. The Still Point, our true nature, accepts every circumstance and condition equally, and if we truly desire peace, we must learn to do the same.

α: *It seems like you are saying that acceptance of all circumstances as they come or complete surrender is the key to happiness, but why is this so difficult?*

Ω: The path of surrender is perfectly legitimate, but until the ego is seen as nonexistent, they are at complete odds. Your true nature of aware presence accepts everything without resistance, while the ego thought system rejects everything either subtly or blatantly. Thus, when you are still aligned with the belief that you are your thoughts and feelings, you are compelled to be in resistance with the now. This is why surrender under these conditions is so difficult. Behavioral control ultimately does not work. You need to see clearly that you are not, nor have you ever been, your thoughts or feelings but instead the open awareness in which they appear. From this recognition, surrender is possible because it is your very nature. This is not to say that practicing surrender during the seeming process of self-inquiry is a bad idea, just that it is in a sense "taking the long way home."

α: *You mention possessing objects is not a problem, but also speak to the rampant consumerism in the world today, so is there not some danger in stressing this?*

Ω: When you know yourself as the Still Point, there is no sense of possession of anything. When there is no separate self, what is there to possess? Objects are what they are and can be utilized and enjoyed as needed. It is only when objects are sought from the belief in being a separate self that the problem arises. Lasting happiness can only come from the knowing of yourself, and once this is clearly understood, there is no remaining confusion about the objective world. It takes care of itself, so to speak.

α: *You mention all the people who have attained worldly fame or material riches only to end their lives in despair. Isn't there an opportunity there to "turn around" and search within?*

Ω: Yes, absolutely! When one reaches the point of realization that nothing in the external world can bring lasting peace and happiness, it presents a wonderful opportunity to look within. Of course, this requires taking the next step, and that can seem painful coming from a place of despair. Those who are willing to take this next step may see that they were in the perfect position for recognizing the Still Point, which not only can never be taken away, but is peace and happiness itself.

α: *Death can seem like the only escape from this level of extreme despair, but does it really solve the problem?*

Ω: The death of the body to the mind that believes it is separate is not death at all but merely a transition. True death can only occur when one has recognized themselves as the Still Point of aware presence. Then the great death begins, which is the "death" of the conditioned ego structures that have kept one imprisoned. In the absence of this recognition, these "energies" consisting of the belief in being a separate isolated entity persist, and after the death of the body, will likely find outlet in another expression of form at some point.

α: *Are you referring to reincarnation?*

Ω: In this "human experience," we have associated our true nature with our bodies and thinking minds, and while we still believe and feel that we are the body, we are bound to form. When the body dies, unless one has clearly recognized their true nature, these energies will, at some point, associate with a different form. This has been extensively described by various traditions as reincarnation, but it's important to understand that "people" don't "reincarnate" as the belief in being a separate person was never true. Describing this process as reincarnation can be helpful as a model, but it serves no purpose to make the mistake of believing in actual separate entities travelling serially through space and time.

20

BE A SEED OF LIGHT IN A DESPERATE WORLD

Because the ego is the belief in being a separate individual entity, it extends this belief outward to all things, especially other people. This is seen and expressed as differences between "us" and "them." We have fractured ourselves into so many different camps that it is almost impossible to describe. We separate based on gender, race, religion, political party, and nationality to name only a few. We invent new reasons to be suspicious of or outright hateful toward others, seeing only the differences between us instead of the reality that we all share the same unified being. This is not only a strategy that will never lead to happiness, but also a strategy that is destroying our planet on many levels. In the twentieth century, the ego reached its fever pitch in the form of outright wars. Wars that directly or indirectly killed hundreds of millions of people over absurd ideologies and nationalistic pride. So far in this new century, the ego's doctrine of "separate to divide" has turned its attention to novel ways of creating and exploiting differences between us with the same devious goal. The only way to end this insanity, and the only hope this planet has of surviving and thriving, is for each individual to "drop out" of the ego's game and return to the recognition of our shared universal being. This is everyone's individual responsibility and the only way to ever find lasting peace and happiness. Even in the early stages of the recognition that we are not our bodies and thinking minds but the awareness in which they appear, we have a responsibility to recognize this awareness belongs to "everyone." The awareness with which we know our everyday experience is the same awareness with which every living being knows their experience as well. Seeing this and living from this understanding will not only change you, but it will also be your blessing to a world that is badly in need of love. This means giving up any participation in the game of separation. Regardless of how anyone lives their life, realize that they too are just trying to find happiness. If others have yet to glimpse our shared reality, it's your goal, as one who has, to lead them there with your loving and completely nonjudgmental actions. This is not a path of preaching or proselytizing but of living this understanding in your daily life. When you live and relate with others as one who is open, accepting, nonjudgmental, and kind, you are providing an example of truth for all to follow. You are truly a blessing to the world, and in the process, you are deepening your felt understanding of the Still Point as the truth of all.

α: *How important is it to cultivate friends who share this understanding, and is it necessary to move away from those who don't?*

Ω: It can be very helpful to spend time with likeminded friends, but your "classroom" in living this understanding is with whomever you are interacting with at any point in time, regardless of their understanding. It will become clear organically if you need to move on from a friendship or other relationship, but there is a danger in stepping out of your classroom too soon, or for the wrong reasons. Any relationship can serve as a source of catalyst to trigger old, egoic conditioning, and many people, instead of eliminating their ego-based reactivity, simply move away from the relationship to accomplish that goal. This is a tactic of avoidance and is not in line with being a true learner.

α: *I've come to find my job meaningless, or perhaps it's more accurate to say I want to move in another direction where my work better expresses this understanding in a way that is helpful to all. Should I just throw caution to the wind and move out of one career and into another?*

Ω: Your "contribution" to this understanding is in your state of being in every moment. Sweeping the floor becomes a sacred act when undertaken from the understanding of the Still Point as our universal shared being. By all means "follow your bliss" in all matters, including the so-called big ones like which line of work to pursue, but never diminish whatever it is you find yourself doing in the present. To sacrifice the actions of now in the hope of performing more useful action in the future is missing the point entirely. Give the now, and whatever actions it entails, your undivided being and you will seamlessly flow into a future that has been perfectly prepared.

α: *So, the type of a job or career one has is not important in expressing or sharing this understanding?*

Ω: No. Undertaking any job, or task for that matter, from a place of understanding one's true nature will mean always coming from a place of love. It doesn't matter what the particulars are, but this world would certainly benefit from those who live this understanding in all walks of life. One of the great sages of the twentieth century, Atmananda Krishna Menon, who was partly responsible for the reemergence of the direct approach to this understanding we have discussed here, was in law enforcement for most of his working life. He was a police inspector and later a district superintendent of police until his retirement. The popular belief that all realized sages spend their lives in a cave, or exclusively living in an ashram, is not true at all. It was said he did his job with perfect compassion and love for all regardless of the actions they committed. Imagine this world if most professions were led by those who lived this understanding. It would look very different than it does today.

α: *I recently heard an author on the science of consciousness claim that the base state of consciousness is not "being aware of being aware." Or to put it another way, consciousness gradually becomes self-aware as individual minds "wake up" to their true reality. Can you explain?*

Ω: Just as the nature of the sun is to shine, the nature of consciousness, or the Still Point, is awareness itself. It is by nature self-aware. There is a trend in contemporary consciousness studies to equate consciousness exclusively with experience, and when experience is absent, to reclassify consciousness in some way such as calling it "the Absolute." In this case, all "relational" aspects of consciousness are absent, and consciousness just is, all by itself so to speak. What is not being clearly seen is that consciousness is always all by itself. There is nothing to experience except consciousness vibrating within itself. This misunderstanding contains within it some remaining belief that we, as human beings, have some independent existence and that consciousness is the product of the brain. It's a slightly evolved materialistic perspective, yet one that ultimately shows the materialist's deep attachment to experience.

α: *If there is no way to experience the absolute, how can it be discussed?*

Ω: In truth, it can't be discussed as no words could ever apply, but you "experience" it every night in deep sleep. There is no conventional experience present and no awareness of having a body or being a person, yet "you" remain. This pristine state is awareness or consciousness simply being itself, which is self-aware. In essence, it is the "I am" relieved of the "I." In this case, the absolute is just another word for the Still Point or consciousness in its "pure" form, meaning without its activity, which we call experience.

α: *What about the cases where there has been brain injury and it has completely changed the subject's personality, yet their consciousness remains intact?*

Ω: The brain is the physical representation of the filtering mechanism of consciousness, or awareness, and when it is damaged by disease or trauma, the filtering is naturally affected. The type or shape of experience may change after having a brain injury, but the knowing of that present experience remains perfectly pristine. The tendency to question the primacy of consciousness versus matter, in this case the brain, is a natural consequence of having remaining materialistic beliefs. Consciousness is eternally "intact" and nothing can ever affect that because there is nothing other than consciousness present.

α: *You mention how insanely divided the world seems to be these days, and it's true that seemingly every day there is a new way to classify or divide us. Why is this the case and what can we collectively do about it?*

Ω: The operating system of the ego or the split mind is one of constant division. Like a river cut off from the ocean, it wanders constantly in search of a home. When humans fail to recognize our collective shared identity, we do the same. The consequence of continual division is isolation, which eventually breeds contempt and aggression toward the "other." This is not a sustainable system and eventually it will collapse on itself. The only solution is to turn around and go within to the Still Point, which is our shared identity. From here, the externals are just that and nothing more. Race, religion, nationality, and all of the other differences that we previously identified will yield to the majestic recognition that we are all completely the same at our core. The nature of this "core" is peace and happiness itself. When you recognize this you save yourself, and when you save yourself you save the world.

21

THE NEVER-ENDING
JOURNEY IN TRUTH

There is a common misperception in spiritual circles that the clear recognition of ourselves as the Still Point, and the all-important realization of its unlimited and ever-present nature, is somehow the end of discovery. It's true that this realization ends the journey to peace and happiness, but it is truly just the beginning of another, more fascinating journey. This "journey" is the unending realignment of the body and mind to this new understanding. As attention is shifted away from the preoccupation with body parts and body systems, the deep contractions of the body relax and it gradually becomes far more open and transparent. The great reduction in repetitive thinking allows the body to be experienced with much greater sensitivity than before. The body still experiences pain and may occasionally get sick, but without the addition of the psychological resistance that normally accompanies illness, it is a much different experience—one that is free of suffering.

In much the same way, the reactivity of the mind to circumstances or situations that previously caused contraction and reaction as a separate self also diminish. This is the gradual release of the deep egoic conditioning that came from the sense of being a separate isolated self that must always be defended. In ways, it is analogous to peeling the layers of a large onion that was built from birth onward by the progressive addition of society's beliefs in separation onto our being. While much of this realignment happens in the process of recognizing the nature of the self-aware Still Point, it continues in perpetuity after that realization is established. However, unlike the difficult and often painful realignment that occurs on the road to this understanding, this process now happens within the backdrop of peace gained from realizing our infinite liberation. While our sense of being—our self-awareness—resides eternally and thus outside of time, our experience within time and space gradually evolves to reflect this new truth. For example, during the three states of waking, dreaming, and deep sleep, aware-being is never "lost" or obscured by either the rapidly changing experience of waking and dreaming, nor the non-experience of deep sleep. When this sense of "being-ness" remains unbroken, the previous fear we held of dissolution becomes impossible. Likewise, during the waking state, our interactions reflect our new understanding. Although we can see much more clearly when other's behavior reflects the confusion of thinking one is a separate, finite entity, we refuse to meet that behavior on the same level. Humility becomes our modus operandi, but it is the humility of being content and knowing that peaceful actions demonstrate understanding in every moment.

α: *Can you say more about the recognition of self during sleeping and waking?*

Ω: When identity has shifted from the belief that we are our bodies and our thoughts and feelings to knowing, not believing, we are the ever-present awareness in which the body and mind appear, we remain anchored continually in the self. At first, we recognize that our aware-being has been present and unchanged during all experiences of our lives. For example, we can think back to certain events and see that while the experience of these events was always changing, our aware-being was always present and always aware. In time, we begin to "switch" our identity from the experiences themselves to that ever-present aware-being. Eventually, when this has established itself, we find that while we are dreaming, our identity remains with the awareness that knows all of the changing aspects of the dream. Finally, this unbroken awareness is recognized as deep sleep itself. There is no experience present, but much like in deep meditation, awareness remains aware only of itself. This is what we have called the Still Point in its pure form.

α: *What is the practice to realize this unbroken awareness during all three states?*

Ω: The practice is to shift one's attention from all that comes and goes, turning away from the veiling power of sights, sounds, thoughts, feelings, and so forth to the awareness that knows them but never comes or goes. This shifting of attention is actually a relaxing of attention, or a complete surrender into the awareness that is the core of our being. Contemplating this deeply and often, both during times of no experience, such as in formal meditation, as well as in the midst of experience, will gradually allow one to shift their identity away from the always changing to the changeless Still Point. In time, this will extend itself into sleep and an unmoving backdrop of peace will forever be present, even while dreaming.

α: *Can you say something about the correct posture for meditation?*

Ω: Meditation is resting knowingly as what you are, the Still Point, and thus can't be affected by posture in any way. By all means, sit in a lotus position if you want, or if circumstances dictate, but never equate the perfect changeless self that you are to be something that can be "attained" or "lost" by anything physical. If one is sitting in meditation and feels pain, it is also perfectly appropriate to shift or move to alleviate the pain. This is not a path of asceticism in any way.

α: *Is the goal of meditation nirvikalpa samādhī, and is that the highest spiritual state one can obtain?*

Ω: Meditation is resting knowingly as the Still Point, your very being. In true meditation there is no meditator, and nothing meditated on, so any concepts such as "goals" do not apply. Nirvikalpa samādhī is simply awareness without any objective components. As the thinking mind dissolves into its source, there may be very pleasant or even blissful experiences, but these are "side effects" in the body and mind as it relaxes into the Still Point. It's important to recognize that this blissful experience is still an experience, and thus some aspect of mind remains active. In what has been called sahaja samādhī, full awareness of the self remains present during all the activities of the waking state. As meditation is what you are and not something you do, the peace of self-awareness in the presence of everyday activities is a higher realization, indicative of the realignment of the body-mind after the clear recognition of our ever-present nature.

THINK AND ACT
ONLY FROM THE
STILL POINT

There is a way to move through the changing world that is forever anchored in the changeless. When we move beyond understanding the Still Point at the level of the thinking mind to feeling it as our very being, we begin to deconstruct the vast, illusory world we have created. We see it was nothing more than a web of thoughts that have solidified over the decades into hard beliefs. We see the insane number of divisions and judgements that we have collectively built around those divisions to be completely false. We recognize that it was fear—fear based upon nonexistent separation—that allowed us to create a world of opposites where we must forever "be on guard" and view our fellow man with suspicion. We fully recognize our very self as the knowing that observes all experience, and while we also realize the changing experience is our substance as well, it is the change-less, observing backdrop that is our forever home. Even in the midst of the most turbulent experiences, the backdrop of peace remains. We recognize that our experience of space and time is a construct of perception and thought respectively. It is only with thinking that ever-present reality seems to become time. Likewise, the act of seeing takes infinite, borderless reality and objectifies it into what seems like space. This understanding reveals that our experience does not take place in space and time, but that space and time take place in our ever-present aware-being. Just as when we dream at night, the entirety of the dreamed world is made entirely of our mind, the entirety of the waking state is also made of nothing but the one mind that is the very substance of all sentient beings. Every thought we have comes from either the knowing of this universal unity, or from the belief in being a separate, individual self. In time, we are able to distinguish the dif-ference between these thoughts easily. If a thought arises on behalf of separation, it can be simply dismissed, as following those thoughts waters the seeds of suffering. The same discrimination can be applied to any actions we take in the world. If they are consistent with the knowing of our one shared being, they are in alignment. If not, they should be avoided as they will never bring peace and happiness but only contribute to misery in the end.

α: *In seeing through the illusion of three-dimensional space, doesn't it take away from the beauty of perception?*

Ω: Seeing through the illusion, even temporarily, is the only way to experience beauty. Beauty is the recognition of the Still Point in relation to objects. It is a "merging" of the one seeing with the object seen so that no distinction remains. You may recall wandering through an art museum when a particular picture catches your eye, and you are "blown away" by beauty. For a time, there is no separation felt but only seeing. No you and no separate picture. In time, the mind reengages you as the observer, but the perfume of awareness remains as beauty.

α: *How can I reconcile eating meat with my understanding of non-duality?*

Ω: Ultimately all "bodies" are made of the same substance. All bodies are nonexistent in that they don't stand out from the awareness in which they are experienced and out of which they are made. Plants too are living "bodies" in this aspect and are capable of their own sentience and communication as well. If this is realized, then it's clear that an artificial distinction at some level is being made. The distinction of where to draw this line is an individual choice based on many factors and is perfectly fine as long as it is made lovingly, and plants and animals are treated without cruelty or unnecessary pain. Regardless of what we choose to eat, we should always express love and thanks to the plants or animals that have played a perfect role in providing nourishment.

α: *I just can't seem to understand how thought creates time, and seeing creates space...*

Ω: It has nothing to do with intellectual understanding but is rather your direct experience. What experience have you ever had that wasn't felt as *here* and *now?* Regardless of where you seem to travel, your feeling is that you are here. It is always "here" no matter if you are on a ship in the middle of the ocean or sitting on your bed at home. Regardless of what sights you are seeing, it feels "here." This is of course the same with time, as it is always "now" in our experience. When you close your eyes in meditation and thought falls away, there is no experience of time or space. Rather the felt "experience" is of just being—here and now. This is the ever-changeless Still Point. It is only when thinking resumes that a sense of time can seem to exist, and likewise when you open your eyes, space also seems to spring into existence. We are so caught up in our beliefs that we default to what the thinking mind tells us about space and time, and we ignore, or miss, the deeper felt reality that lies just under the surface regardless of what we are thinking or seeing. This is why we equate the unawakened state as living almost exclusively in our thoughts, which are misty and dreamlike, in that they seem to obscure the underlying reality at their core.

α: *I have heard some teachers refer to receiving guidance that is sometimes quite specific from the Holy Spirit or the higher self. Is this something that actually happens?*

Ω: While all thoughts arise from the Still Point, which is the undivided ground of our being, those that are filtered through a strong sense of separation will often be less than helpful. The discrimination one gains in recognizing, and immediately discarding, thoughts arising on behalf of separation is part of one's spiritual evolution. Thoughts, and the actions they inspire, that come from separation will either subtly or grossly defend or assist the concept of being a separate, unique person. Right minded thoughts and actions that arise only from whole being are inclusive of the best interests of all, without division. Following only thoughts that arise from our undivided being can produce a state of "flow" in which any concept of a felt individualized "doer" is absent.

The Still Point, or Holy Spirit, is always offering the seemingly separate self the gift of grace. That is to say a pull from ourselves to return to ourselves is always in play for those who have the eyes to see and the ears to hear.

α: *Is there a practical way to determine if the origin of a thought was the split (egoic) mind or unified mind?*

Ω: The split mind is fear, while the unified mind is love. For example, if a thought of worry or concern about some imagined future event arises, you can be certain it's coming from the split mind and can be immediately dropped. If it's a practical matter pertaining to the future, such as remembering to put a meeting you have scheduled into your calendar, then of course proceed. It's very important not to try to control your thoughts in any way, but it is absolutely your choice of whether to "follow" them or not. So as thoughts arise freely, any that come from fear, or the split mind, can be happily ignored.

α: *My "best" or most illuminating meditations seem to be those that are unplanned. For example, when I am sitting on the couch reading or watching TV and I get the sudden urge to meditate, I have a more peaceful and revealing experience. Does this make any sense?*

Ω: Alan Watts once said, "When one is trying to outwit the devil it's terribly important not to give him any advance notice." There is truth to this in the early stages of what you call meditation because the default mode of the split mind that believes in separation is frantic thinking. The egoic split mind will do anything to avoid being seen as it truly is, and thoughts will arise that seem to implore you to follow them. The other tactic the ego mind will use is to draw one into sleep so as to miss the clear recognition of the Still Point as our essential being. When one unexpectedly relaxes their attention and rests as awareness, the mind can be caught off-guard if you will. In time, as we return over and over again to resting as our aware-being, thoughts gradually lose their power to pull us into their web, and the clear distinction between what we are as awareness, and what arises from awareness as thought, is clearly seen.

α: *Sometimes I don't feel comfortable using words that reinforce separation or duality and I use other words, but it can feel awkward. Such as instead of saying, "I love you," I will say, "We are love." My friends look at me funny, so do you have any advice?*

Ω: There is as much duality in saying "we are love" as in "I love you." Regardless, as the ACIM teacher Ken Wapnick used to say, just be normal. There is no need to try and out-think yourself or to create some unique, spiritual lexicon to use in polite company. We all know how to act normally and acting normally is the most polite and most loving thing to do for all present.

α: *When I was studying* **A Course in Miracles,** *I went through a period of very dark, difficult dreams. Now that I have been on the direct path, I notice I seem to awaken after a few hours of sleeping and have a very difficult time falling back asleep. It's becoming a problem, and I'm wondering if there is anything to do?*

Ω: Periods of sleep disturbance, as you describe, are quite common as we start to seriously look at the conditioned ego beliefs we have held. The nightmares can be understood as a slow "draining" of the deep unconscious beliefs that "ascend" to more accessible, superficial layers of the mind during sleep. Likewise, early waking with difficulty falling back asleep is also common at times on this path. Although challenging for practical purposes, they are very much signs of true progress and should be understood and accepted as such. Instead of resisting these periods, take the opportunity to "meditate" or contemplate them as the awareness you are. The opportunity to rest knowingly as awareness during the transition from the waking to the dream state, and deep sleep to the waking state, can be very revealing.

THE POWER OF
UNDERSTANDING
PRECEEDING ACTION

The early Christian mystic St. Augustine once said, "Love and do what you will." If understood correctly, this is one of the most profound teachings ever put into words on how to live life. Another way of saying this would be to understand your true self-aware nature as the one self-aware nature of all sentient beings and allow that realization to dictate all actions you take, or do not take, in the world. Love is itself the recognition of the one shared being that we all are at our core. When we experience the feeling of love—such as with a romantic partner, a friend, or a pet—we are actually seeing through the outward form of the "beloved" to the underlying unity of our joint being. The way in which we interact with a romantic partner and a pet may be very different, but the actual feeling of love is exactly the same. We see and feel ourselves in them even though our external forms appear different. Likewise, when we say we have fallen out of love with someone, in reality all we are doing is contracting back into a sense of separation or separateness as love itself—the joint ground of our being neither comes nor goes or changes in any way. The way we act toward each other when "in love" is very different than when that feeling is absent. When "in love," we treat each other as we would like to be treated with kindness, compassion, and complete equality as hallmarks of our interactions. With the recognition that our own self-aware being is the same self-aware being of all sentient creatures, the way we see so-called others and the outside world radically changes. You then profoundly understand that "as you do unto others you do unto yourself." Further on, as this realization becomes established, you begin to not just understand this, but you begin to feel it implicitly as well. Even during the phase where this is simply understood, you begin to see that treating everyone as if they are your very self allows happiness and peace to move into the forefront of your experience. Treating others as yourself is an absolute truth that is recognized by the universe and extends benefits to you, benefits that were previously withheld by actions not in alignment with our source. Concepts like war, murder, or enslavement of any kind, be it economic or otherwise, are seen as the type of pure unconscious insanity that is completely "harming" the perpetrators ultimately even more then the so-called victims. One can never find actual happiness while still believing these actions have some "value" for them in any way. You may possess extreme amounts of wealth or power, but you will never find true happiness and freedom until you see and embody this clearly. Even thinking that one can escape or reset this after death is sheer folly. These self-serving energies will eventually find outlet in another form, and the misery of learning the lesson will begin anew until the truth of our one undivided being is seen and embraced. Only then will freedom be forever gained.

α: *Doesn't saying that "self-serving energies will find outlet in another form" speak to reincarnation directly?*

Ω: It's saying that unresolved attachment to form, meaning that the amalgamation of pure awareness with experience, such as bodily sensations and thoughts, have not yet been teased apart. As such, the belief that one's identity is still a body-mind is intact. The "energies" of this belief are not consistent with the complete stillness of our true, undivided nature and will eventually, when combined with other unresolved similar energies, associate with a new form. This is, in essence, as "choiceless" as a wayward stream that continues to make its way to find the ocean.

α: *At some level of spiritual understanding, can this reassociation with bodily form, after death, become a choice?*

Ω: It seems plausible that one who has seen completely through the illusion of form can choose to "appear" as form again for teaching purposes to help others gain this recognition. To be clear, because there was no "person" left when the body was laid down, there is no "person" reappearing, only empty aware-being associating as form so as to facilitate communication. This possibility could be called a deep intuition, but not something with which I have direct experience. Of course, much attention has been given to this by certain traditions, such as in Tibetan Buddhism.

α: *So, if one prioritizes love, how we act and what we do in the world will take care of itself?*

Ω: Prioritize knowing yourself as the Still Point first and others will be known as the same. This love moves beyond any sense of lack and eliminates looking for others to "complete you." When we enter into special relationships, we give the "other" the impossible task of fulfilling us. When we proceed from the recognition of our one shared being, our actions lack neediness and true intimacy dawns.

α: *My son is going through a very difficult time with depression and addiction and I don't know if he is going to survive. Is there a way to introduce this understanding to him?*

Ω: Demonstrating this understanding through your loving actions is the only option until he "turns around" of his own volition. Any time we try to force someone to stop and look within, it will either have no effect or can even be counterproductive. It must be each and every person's personal recognition to clearly see that happiness can't be found in external experience of any kind. By all means, be loving and supportive, providing whatever resources you can for his safety, but recognize that we can only do so much as this is always, ultimately, an individual journey.

α: *What is addiction in terms of this understanding?*

Ω: Addiction is relentlessly chasing the Still Point in the one place it can never be found, experience. At some point an experience, be it a drug, alcohol, sex, or whatever, resulted in a glimpse of the peace and happiness of our true nature. Instead of recognizing that the drug or experience caused desire to temporarily drop away, we wrongly believe it was the experience itself that caused the deep feeling of peace to surface. We then chase that feeling of profound relief with ever-increasing quantities of the substance, or experience, but to no avail. We fail to see that it was the state of being without desire that was the cause of the contentment. At the point where we see that the experience can never bring lasting happiness, we either look to other experiences to make us happy and we remain in misery, or we finally turn around and look within.

α: *Is it necessary to go into "retreat" to help establish the understanding of our true nature?*

Ω: The Still Point of aware-being is what you are, now and always. Nothing can be said to be necessary to see this other than to remove the blocks that are obstructing its recognition. But because those blocks are constructed by losing ourselves in experience, the practice of "retreating" from the roller coaster of experience can be very valuable. Most people are deeply attached to the concept of psychological time, and that attachment makes it very difficult to live in the "now." Retreating from habitual schedules for a time can begin to loosen that attachment. It's also extremely valuable to "unplug" from the constant stream of misinformation so commonly pumped into society today. Of course, it's important if you join a group to retreat, you do so with a teacher who is established in this understanding and who relentlessly points you back to the recognition of your true nature.

α: *Why did you choose to write much of this book in a Q&A format?*

Ω: It would be more accurate to say it chose to be written this way. Very few of the questions were asked by outside parties. In a sense, they were all direct questions or variants of questions I myself had during my path to understanding. I can say there is immense power in a genuine question. The question and the answer come from the same placeless place, but the question is filtered through the belief system of the mind asking it, which makes it very unique. In the purest sense, this direct path approach to the understanding of our true nature "lives" in a question-and-answer format. At its heart the teaching is an oral tradition best suited to one-on-one dialogue in the moment. Even the written word is a bit of a distillation, but in any event, the quality of the question begets the quality of the answer.

α: *Are there stages or steps of understanding that can be described on the spiritual journey as sort of a map or a guidebook?*

Ω: The first step, if we can call it that, is the recognition that one is not the body-mind, but rather the aware-presence that knows the experiences of the body and the mind. This instant, often a flash of understanding, is a timeless occurrence as you, aware presence, are timeless as well. The hallmarks of this discovery are quite profound, and often intellectually transformative, but not yet fully liberating as this awareness is still felt to be personal. Just as we know that our thoughts and bodily feelings are uniquely ours, we continue to superimpose this limitation onto awareness and believe it is also unique to us as individuals. We call it "our awareness," if you will. Because of this misconception, a subtle fear of lack or death can still remain.

The second step, which eventually dawns with repeated immersion into this newly evident aware presence, is the recognition that this awareness is not personal—not your awareness, but universal awareness that is ever-present and without borders or boundaries of any kind. This is the truly liberating realization traditionally called enlightenment, or salvation. With this realization, the discovery moves beyond something understood intellectually to something felt on every level of being. Here it is seen that while you are having a unique "human" experience, the only "real" or lasting aspect is this aware presence without which no experience could ever be had. With this realization, it is still initially possible to have feelings that were previously identified as fear but because they have no basis in belief to grasp onto, they quickly dissipate.

The final stage is not really a stage in that it doesn't end. This is the ongoing realignment of all aspects of experience to conform with our new profound understanding. How we think, feel, act, and interact with others and the world beautifully unfolds in this now seamless background of peace.

α: *So even after the recognition of our true nature being indestructible, we can still experience fear or anxiety?*

Ω: When the nature of our self as the Still Point of aware presence is clearly seen, along with the clear recognition of its ever-present and infinite nature, some aspects of the previous deep conditioning of the body and mind remain.

It's possible that bodily sensations that the mind previously labeled as fear or anxiety can arise, but they are no longer supported by the concomitant thoughts that gave them their "bite," so to speak. As such, they are felt as completely neutral waves of vibration in awareness and can't rightly be called fear or anxiety anymore. In fact, because they are completely accepted, with no thought added, they may even feel pleasant. Regardless, because they are not reinforced in any way, they quickly fade and appear less and less frequently over time.

α: *What remains then?*

Ω: Open transparent awareness remains. Experience continues to arise in this open awareness, but thought no longer "reaches out" and tries to push away or resist experiences previously labeled "bad" or "undesirable," and it no longer tries to hold onto or seek experiences previously labeled "good" or "pleasurable."

THE INABILITY TO JUDGE WITHIN THE EXPERIENCE OF SPACE AND TIME

The heart of most of the great religious and spiritual traditions of the world contain teachings of nonjudgement and forgiveness. There is great wisdom in these teachings because it is completely impossible to judge anything when coming from a belief in separation. We fail to see it is the very belief that we are separate individual entities that is the prerequisite for suffering itself. Such questions as, "Why are there people in the world suffering so much more than me?" becomes a statement of belief instead of an actual question. The very question contains the assumption that there are in fact "others" and that they are suffering "more." And while that may be relatively true, what if that suffering compels them to "wake up" to the recognition of our shared universal being? In that case, was not suffering a blessing in disguise? It is simply not possible from this perspective to see the unity of all experience, or to judge it as good or bad, better or worse. As *A Course in Miracles* states, "Judgement is not our function." This never implies that we condone suffering or unconscious actions on the part of others, but we must refrain from judging them. When no judgement has been applied, the concept of forgiveness, in the traditional sense, is no longer necessary. As the clarity that we all are the Still Point dawns, it also becomes clear, in moments of great insight, that every event or circumstance in our lives happened exactly when and how it did in order to "nudge" us, or even "shove" us, toward the recognition of our true nature. This applies to all events, but especially those considered difficult or challenging. We also see that while we did not always respond to these challenges in the most beneficial way, any lesson not learned would simply need to be repeated at another time. There is a tremendous release in this understanding. We recognize the entire reason for this experience in space and time is to discover ourselves as the timeless and changeless awareness in which space and time itself appears.

α: *What does this say about us having free will?*

Ω: You have the ultimate free will in that it is always your choice to come from either fear or love, separation or unity. This extends to the interpretation of any seeming event on the "screen" of life. The Still Point, your very being, accepts all appearances and circumstances without resistance or clinging of any kind. This is the position of love. It is taking your stand as the open awareness that you are, which is devoid of judgement. Any resistance or clinging to experience implies operating from fear, or the belief in separation. There is no "middle ground" to speak of here. In essence, it is a binary choice.

α: *To a child that does not understand non-duality, what would you tell them is real?*

Ω: If asked, I would tell them love is real. I would point out that the feeling of love they have for their parent, friend, or pet is exactly the same if they really explore it. Regardless of the "object" of their love, the feeling is the same. Expounding on that would depend on the particular child and circumstances of their life and upbringing, but even children raised to believe exclusively in being a separate individual can understand the unity in the feeling of love.

α: *You've said not to control your thoughts during meditation, but I don't understand why.*

Ω: What would try to control the mind but the mind itself? The Still Point, your true nature, controls nothing, limits nothing, adds nothing to any experience, including thought. Meditation is being that which you already are, the Still Point. So, if there is any attempt to control the mind, it is a movement away from your true nature and thus counterproductive. Simply allow thoughts to come and go without "attaching" to them or following them in any way. You will see the only "substance" to a thought is the unlimited sea of consciousness from which it arises and falls back into.

α: *There is so much fear in the world today, how is it possible to overcome this?*

Ω: It is always only possible to recognize yourself as the Still Point, which is love itself, and thus forever abandon fear as your operating system. When you do so, it also has the greatest effect on the human collective as possible because that recognition is not personal. The very being you now understand as "all that you are" is also known as the one unified being of all sentient life. It's true that our society is highly agitated these days, but that is the natural state of a system that is about to undergo a phase transition. In this case from fear to love. There are enough people on earth who have recognized, to various depths, that we are all one universal being appearing as many different viewpoints. At this point of "critical spiritual mass" you are seeing the collective agitation and unrest that is the death throes of a civilization moving from fear to love, chaos to peace. That's why it is critical that you recognize your true nature and assist everyone else in doing the same, by your example.

α: *My best friend is involved with a group studying non-duality, but her guru insists the teaching is ancient and must remain shrouded in secrecy for the good of the students. Basically, only the guru can initiate them, and they can't describe the techniques they use unless the guru "clears them" to do so. Does this make sense?*

Ω: What could possibly be more free or open than the simple recognition of what we already always are, aware presence? When the question "Are you aware?" is asked and you pause, say yes, and remain as that awareness, you are engaged in the highest spiritual undertaking possible. What is secret about that in any way? The simple awareness that you are is the supreme guru itself. Over time, it reveals all that is needed when one knowingly rests as that alone. Now it's true that some people who are very identified with the personal self are not ready for the knowledge that the world they so believed in is not as it seems, and that can have unwanted psychological consequences, but those are very rare cases. In general, this simple, direct approach is very applicable to the needs of the world today.

α: *What about the teaching of siddhis, or special powers?*

Ω: Being happy and living without fear is a special power. It's certainly true that with special dedicated training, many things are possible, but they don't necessarily equate to knowing your true nature and its inherent qualities. That is not to say there have not been those who were well established in the understanding of their true nature who also had special abilities, such as healing, and so forth, but the "goal" of the direct path—in fact the goal of all spirituality—is the knowing of your true unlimited nature and the dissolution of the deep egoic conditioning that has kept one in chains of bondage.

α: *What does non-duality say about what information we can trust?*

Ω: Ultimately the only aspect of experience that can be trusted, in that it is completely changeless, is the Still Point, our self-aware being. All other knowledge, information, or experience is relational, and is relatively "true" or "false" based on a collective agreement. This, of course, doesn't mean we never accept information from "trusted" sources, but nothing beats raw, direct experience. As one's discrimination vastly increases, you will see that many of the sources people have been conditioned to trust are completely mired in egoic fearmongering. This is to keep people afraid and compliant.

Because the spiritual mass of this world is increasing, so is the ability of many to discriminate when they are being fed fear-based lies to support an egoic agenda. It's why you see more and more people waking up to reject the old party line, which only wants separation and division.

α: *What is the connection or common link between yoga for the purpose of self-realization and the very prevalent Hatha yoga, of stretching and poses, seen all over the world today?*

Ω: I am not a historian of the evolution or devolution of ancient yogic systems, but the Sanskrit root of yoga means to "join" or "yoke." In essence, yoga is the science of merging the so-called personal consciousness into the one universal or pure consciousness that is its only true reality. It's easy to see how the application of Hatha yoga, as a form of mostly physical exercise and stretching, came from the early tantric schools that did not shy away from including the body and the world in this investigation of our true nature. The difference is the tantric approach had no outward goal, such as the beautification or flexibility of the body, but only the inclusion of sensation and perception to recognize their ever-present and unlimited source of universal consciousness, the self. This does not mean to undermine the value of Hatha yoga in any way, but rather to point out that it serves a different purpose from what we are discussing here.

THE ULTIMATE
GURU

In every moment, you already are. Any thought that arises does so against this background of pure aware-being that is your very nature. When you speak, the sound that is produced arises from, and is known by, your very being. When thinking and speaking cease, you remain. The ever-present Still Point, your very self, is the eternally present background of all experience. The greatest or most pleasurable experiences you have ever had were known by this, as were the most painful. Those experiences came and went, but you, aware-being, always remain. Recognizing this imperturbable being as your very self, what you have always called "I," is a magically definitive step in human spiritual evolution. It is amazing that most humans go through life without this simple recognition. We are so completely mesmerized by the continually changing landscape of external experience, seemingly given concrete reality by memory, that we ignore the true treasure trove of unchanging being at its core. We, in essence, ignore our very self. Our lives are spent wandering through the ever-shifting sands of ephemeral experience, looking for the solidity of happiness and fulfillment in the one place it can never be found. With all of our ambitions for peace tuned to the external, we invariably miss the incomparably sublime reservoir of internal peace itself, without which no experience could ever be had. Our actions in the world are often driven by desires and fears and are thus rarely spontaneous or clear. Believing our identity is only our "personhood," which is made exclusively of always shifting thoughts and feelings, we wonder why we are perpetually anxious and unfulfilled. We believe memory, itself utterly unreliable, is the underlying unity of our temporary thoughts and feelings. We fail to see that memory is nothing but a thought about something we call the past that we are having in the present. We attempt to build a stable identity around memory, which is just as temporary as the thoughts, feelings, and images to which it refers. We wander in the desert of changing human experience, expecting it will one day deliver lasting peace and happiness. We seek the stable in the perpetually changing and wonder why it never comes.

The instant we recognize the completely stable and unchanging nature of the Still Point, our aware-being, a hint of possibility is gained. The moment we make the connection between what we have always called "I" and the vast ocean of desireless being at our core, a threshold has been crossed. In this instant, we recognize the true continuity of life. We see memory for the grand illusion it always was. We still surely possess memory, and call on it as needed, but never again allow it to convince us that we are merely changing thoughts or feelings. As we begin to leave our thoughts and feelings alone, there is a subtle shift of our felt identity to the Still Point. Our ever-present being emerges from the background into the foreground, while thoughts and feelings are seen and felt as temporary colorings of our true natural self. From this point on, there is a small but exceedingly important change to our notion of spirituality, or our search for lasting happiness. Now, instead of the mind continually searching for truth within its own confines, the truth itself has been glimpsed as the never-changing backdrop in which the mind dances and then rests. Our practice now becomes continually returning or relaxing our attention into this indescribable ocean of awareness. We first do this in what we call meditation. Then, in the midst of our daily experiences we begin to refer back often to that which knows the experiences we are having. When thoughts and feelings evoke fear or anxiety, returning to our peaceful, oceanic being exposes them for the limited temporary energies that they are. Over time, experience loses its ability to distract us from the unshakable peace of our being. The Still Point, our very being, begins to reveal its limitless qualities to us. In truth, we now have only one placeless place that plays the role of the supreme teacher or guru. We have returned home.

α: *If as you say, the thinking mind cannot know the truth of our being, what is its role in the self-realization process?*

Ω: The mind, in the form of thinking and imagining is the limited activity of the unlimited awareness that we are. Asking the mind to understand its source is akin to asking isolated drops of water to "know" or understand the ocean. While there is nothing to thoughts and images other than awareness, the limited or finite can never apprehend the unlimited or infinite. This is not to diminish thinking in any way, because ultimately the mind must come to its own highest level of understanding, in this case, of its limitations, in order for most people to accept their identity fully as the aware-being at the source of mind. In essence, the primacy we previously granted to the thinking mind must yield or shift to the ocean of consciousness that is its actual source.

α: *If the Still Point is ultimately the true teacher or guru, what is the role of human teachers?*

Ω: To relentlessly point you back to the being that they have discovered as their very self, knowing that it is your very self as well.

α: *Can you say something about the specifics of your own path to this understanding?*

Ω: My path was one of relationship. One day, in the midst of constant and destructive seeking for happiness in all things "out there," I met someone and felt an instant flash of recognition and love. She felt the very same, and we embarked on a relationship that was both wonderful and terrible in rapid succession. Our egoic identification was both very solid and seemingly often in utter opposition. After a short time, with serious interludes of conflict, we came across *A Course in Miracles* and began to study it together. For the next decade, our understanding of non-duality increased, and some progress was made in our relationship, but serious conflict remained. At one point, after living apart for a year and a half, I clearly recognized, to my disdain at the time, that nothing short of complete dissolution of egoic conditioning would suffice for a true and lasting happy relationship. At the peak of what the world would call a successful career, I left full-time employment and we moved into relative seclusion. Within three days of moving, I found the direct path and our lives became a sort of living retreat, dedicated to this understanding in all ways, for years. My wife shares this living understanding as we walked the path side-by-side until no questions remained.

α: *Is the recognition that we are that aware-being that knows our experience a dramatic event?*

Ω: This recognition, the first peace, is not an event in that it has none of the objective qualities you find in experience. It is, in essence, timeless, as what you essentially are is not located in time. Even in those who experience this understanding suddenly, it's only the reaction of the body and mind to the recognition itself that may seem dramatic. For most people, it's quite easy to recognize awareness, but the sense of identity we have with thoughts and feelings is too great to allow us to accept that we are this awareness. It takes repeated immersion, or resting as the Still Point of being, for the mind to surrender its resistance, in most cases.

"The first peace, which is the most important, is that which comes within the souls of people when they realize their relationship, their oneness with the universe and all its powers, and when they realize that at the center of the universe dwells the Great Spirit, and that this center is really everywhere, it is within each of us."

~ BLACK ELK

α: *You mention relational knowledge or worldly knowledge as being different from the absolute knowledge of the Still Point, so what does this understanding do to our abilities regarding relational or worldly knowledge?*

Ω: The Still Point, as pure unlimited consciousness, is itself intelligent infinity. This is using the word "intelligent" because of its inherent "knowing" or self-aware quality. Any experience that has ever been had by any seeming entity in any universe ever experienced has been known in and by this unlimited "intelligent" awareness. However, for this omnipresent awareness—as pure consciousness—to know specific information, it must first seem to contract into an individuated point of view from whose vantage point it can know or experience certain aspects of itself. This is why in the dream state, despite the fact that there is nothing present but the mind of the dreamer, an "entity" arises from whose point of view the dream is experienced. As this contraction is released in deep sleep, much like a telescope lens that has been defocused, specifics can no longer be viewed or experienced. At this point, awareness is aware only of itself as peace and happiness.

α: *I mean with regard to the mind that has had this clear recognition of self as pure being. Is it able to obtain relational knowledge more easily?*

Ω: The process of learning new "things" is the same in that attention must be focused on whatever subject one is interested in learning. It's true that the mind, in the form of thinking, is not in a state of turbulence or chatter, so in that way the learning process may be experienced as relatively easier. When specific questions are being answered, the answer does not proceed from memory. The question is heard in the Still Point, and the answer proceeds from the Still Point. The words and concepts conveyed are still in harmony with the configuration of the mind filtering them. For example, any answer I give will use concepts and language that reflect the previous relative knowledge that this mind has accumulated. I won't start speaking Russian, or use concepts from, say, the perspective of engineering as I've not studied them.

α: *You mention the need of shifting the primacy from the thinking mind to the consciousness that is its source, but how can there be primacy in perfect oneness or non-duality?*

Ω: There cannot, but from the viewpoint of the separate self, which imagines it is an actual entity, it is appropriate to make this statement. You see, the ego, or separate self, can only seem to exist when its identity is aligned with the ever-changing forms of experience. All experience actually, but thinking and feeling primarily, as even by conventional standards, they are experienced as happening within us. When self-identity is shifted to the completely still backdrop, aware-being, the ego is seen to be completely nonexistent. At this point, the implied duality collapses and is seen only as a teaching tool.

α: *It seems that politics in the West have degraded into a poisonous system of character assassination and pure vitriol. How did we get here, and what is the way out?*

Ω: Modern political systems in the West reflect the mandate of the predominantly ego-based beliefs of the population— namely separating to divide. Any sane, rational society would never begin with separation into two or more "parties" as the starting point for just governance. The understanding of the shared nature of all people should be a prerequisite for leadership in society. When this is not the case, and one sees themselves as being separate, they must see others as separate as well. This is a universal law. The correction for this is for humanity to meet in the middle, at the Still Point. It is necessary for those charged with making decisions involving our planet and its inhabitants to clearly see and know that we all share the same being. Lasting, stable peace between individuals and nations can only be achieved when growing numbers of people, especially in leadership roles, come to this clear understanding.

26

THE PATHOLOGIC
MOVEMENT OF MIND

It's clear to most people that they have a limited span of attention. When concentrating our attention on a particular subject, it's not usually long before the mind wanders off into the past or the future for something more "interesting" to ponder. Every student who has ever prepared for a school exam is likely familiar with this waning lack of ability to focus attention. What is not as obvious to humans is that our span of "inattention" is even less. Novice meditators often find this out very quickly as they first sit to meditate. Their minds simply refuse to cooperate as thoughts assail them almost continually. These thoughts arise in such rapid succession, and are often accompanied by correlating images, that it seems nearly impossible to recognize the pure field of stillness from which they arise. The reason for this is not the thoughts themselves, but the fact that we have been relentlessly conditioned to give attention to these thoughts. We believe, in essence, that we are our thinking minds and thus thoughts must be "followed" regardless of how rational or irrational they are. In fact, most people believe that their thoughts are a major part of their identity. They believe, and more importantly feel, that their thoughts are not only produced by them, but that they are essential to them. They believe if their brain became still and thought ceased, they would not be fully themselves. This could not be further from the truth. In fact, true peace can never be experienced until we recognize the vast, silent Still Point from which all thoughts arise. The Still Point is that which knows the thoughts that arise. When you say, "I know my thoughts," you are correct because you are this vast self-aware Still Point. No thought has any ability to know itself, yet most people believe thoughts to be aware of themselves. Because of this, thoughts are closely followed while the awareness that is your true self, from which they arise and are known, is completely ignored. When thought arises from the timeless Still Point, a sense of passing time accompanies them. There can be no felt sense of time without thinking. In deep sleep, where thought is absent, time is not experienced. This is why it is completely essential to recognize the vast, peaceful field from which thought arises as being ever present and aware. This is meant to say that only the Still Point is aware. Any sensation, thought, or image you have ever experienced was known exclusively by this vast, silent presence. When you come to see this and recognize it is what you have called "I" your entire life, you recognize you are not your thoughts, and they are certainly not essential to you. You "are" before, during, and after thoughts have come and gone. This is the very seed of freedom from the false chains of the thinking mind. Thoughts do not need to be controlled or censored in any way, but simply allowed to rise and fall inside your vast aware-being.

α: *I've heard some teachers say that intense single-pointed concentration of mind is needed to see and experience the self, but this seems in opposition to what you are saying here...*

Ω: Just as prior to falling asleep, a relaxing of attention is necessary, true meditation is akin to falling asleep while remaining aware. Not aware of anything objective, such as thoughts or images, but simply aware of awareness itself. It's true that in many progressive paths to self-realization, a single-pointed attention is achieved before the "final object" is consumed in the vast ocean of awareness, here called the Still Point. In this direct approach to knowing ourselves, we go directly to the recognition that we are the Still Point. Concentration is needed to focus awareness on anything objective, but no concentration is needed for one to know what they always and already are.

α: *You mentioned how memory serves to give us a false sense of continuity of mind, but doesn't memory reside in the Still Point?*

Ω: The Still Point remembers nothing but cannot forget itself. As such, memory is a function of the thinking mind, but not an inherent quality of your self-aware being. The Still Point, your true nature, simultaneously knows, accepts, and releases any experience that arises. Clinging to or resisting any experience is only for the thinking mind, and never your true self. This is why it is often said that the ego is nothing but the activity of seeking and resisting.

α: *You mention humans having a very short span of inattention, but why is this so?*

Ω: Most people are unknowingly addicted to objective experience, so their attention is constantly facing "outward" on sights and sounds, or "inward" only to thoughts and feelings, but almost never on the aware backdrop that knows them. If you contemplate this, you will see this to be the case. This is especially true with thinking as the mind is in constant movement from thought to thought without ceasing. For many people who have yet to "turn around" and deeply contemplate their true nature, only deep sleep gives them a nightly respite from this continual attention on thought forms. The undisciplined or ego mind maintains its illusion of primacy of "being what you are" by remaining in motion. In essence, this continual motion serves to obscure or block your true identity as the Still Point, which lies just under or behind the mind. In reality the Still Point is never obscured because without your ability to know the thoughts that are arising, they would not exist. Once this is clearly seen, even once, you have sowed the seed of liberation from complete identification with the thinking mind.

α: *What about the self-help practice of changing the content of your thoughts, so as to think better thoughts. Is this helpful?*

Ω: Your true nature, what you actually are, knows all thoughts regardless of their content. Good thoughts, bad thoughts, irrational thoughts, or rational thoughts all arise from and are known by yourself, the self-aware Still Point. The only way to ultimately "solve" the problem of the continually chattering mind is to see that you are the Still Point from which the mind, as thought, arises. Only in this way will the mind melt into its source and find the indescribable peace for which it has been searching since the dawn of time.

α: *If the Still Point is what we truly are and it is always present and effortless, why does there seem to be so much effort required to recognize this?*

Ω: As long as your self-identity rests with your body, mind, and senses, there will seem to be effort to recognize your true self from which thinking and feeling arise. In other words, as long as you feel yourself to be a separate, individual entity you will feel effort is being made to reach the effortless. In reality, you, the Still Point, are completely fulfilled effortlessness itself. In time, as this is clearly recognized, resting as your true self will become effortless, and only moving away from this, into thinking and feeling, will seem to require effort.

α: *How does the practice of meditation evolve as the understanding of our true nature increases and becomes more obvious?*

Ω: Formal meditation, or contemplating the aware backdrop of all experience, is useful and necessary while one still feels and believes they are a separate, individuated being. In time, as it becomes clearer that this ever-present awareness is your real self, maintaining your stance as the aware presence you are in the midst of all experience becomes a continual, ongoing affair. The inability of experience—regardless of how turbulent or triggering—to draw you away from your peaceful core becomes the true measure of spiritual progress. This is an ongoing process that never ends.

α: *So then in time, it's not as much about recognizing your true self but living in accordance with that understanding during normal everyday life?*

Ω: Yes, for most of us who choose to live regular lives in the world, abiding from and as the Still Point during all the daily ups and downs we face is the challenge and the reward of having understood the nature of our true being. This is only possible when we have aligned ourselves to ourselves enough to be generally rooted in presence. If our peace is easily disturbed by "difficult" experiences, it remains a conditional peace. Meaning simply that we are still relying on outside circumstances to be a certain way for us to feel peaceful and happy.

α: *What is meant by "living a regular life"?*

Ω: Historically many who have pursued this understanding, or indeed have glimpsed or are even established in it, have chosen to live lives in relative isolation—in an ashram, as a monk in a monastery, or even a cave in the Himalayas, for example. Others who live more conventional lives in the world, with jobs and families, always have the gift of worldly experiences to serve as a test of their understanding. When experiences, especially those we label as difficult or challenging, fail to pull us away from our peaceful nature, we are making true progress.

α: *What are the benefits of this "direct path" approach to self-realization, and why is it helpful for the world we live in today?*

Ω: The fact that it takes one directly to the felt sense of being aware is its prime advantage. In addition, the direct path is devoid of any cultural or societal attachments, and as such it is not relegated to a certain country, culture, language, or lifestyle. Anyone under any circumstance can "go to and abide as" their true nature of awareness once it has been recognized. In essence, it dispenses with any obligatory sense of ritual which seems to be in line with the direction of our evolving modern society.

α: *Do animals such as pets have the ability to progress spiritually or even become realized?*

Ω: Every sentient being on this planet, or any planet for that matter, is already and always the self-aware Still Point at their core. It's true that for most animals, including most humans today, their aware-being is almost completely masked by or merged into their experience. Domestic dogs and cats are far more rooted in their being, or the "now," than most humans. This is why they are such loving and forgiving companions, always ready to enjoy what the moment presents. It would be shortsighted to believe that there could be no spiritual evolution in the animal kingdom. In fact, the great Indian sage Ramana Maharshi declared a cow named

Lakshmi, who came to live at his ashram, to be fully realized before her death, as one example.

α: *So, pets have the same awareness at their core as humans?*

Ω: Dogs, cats, trees, or humans do not have awareness. Awareness has dogs, cats, humans, trees, and so on. This is hard to grasp when one still identifies themselves with their personality and the body. The Still Point, or awareness, is all that is aware. Awareness is self-aware. There are not multiple awarenesses, but one dimensionless self-aware reality in which all experience occurs, and out of which all experience is made. When we refer to concepts like spiritual evolution, we are speaking only of the mind. The Still Point is whole, complete, and utterly changeless. Concepts such as evolution can never apply.

α: *You mention the Still Point lies just under or behind the mind, but if we are speaking of non-duality or oneness, how can this be?*

Ω: The moment we use words, we are in duality. Language is a symbol that can only serve to point to truth. If we wanted absolute accuracy, we would need to remain silent. There is nothing to thoughts other than the knowing or awareness of them, but it's helpful initially to "sparse out" the awareness or knowing aspect as the witness of the mind. Once this is abundantly clear, it can begin to be seen that there is nothing but the awareness or knowing presence at all. The thought, or the sight or sound, is only knowing or awareness vibrating within itself. This collapse into non-duality is the final step in understanding.

α: *I'm still not getting the idea that humans and animals are not aware. Can you explain?*

Ω: The deep materialistic conditioning we have all received trained us to believe that we are our bodies and our minds. As such, we retain the belief that our consciousness is a byproduct of the brain. This results in the confusion of believing that humans and animals have or possess awareness or consciousness. When we see clearly that only awareness is aware and that we are that awareness, then we recognize that the experiences of the body and the mind appear only within awareness. This is why it is accurate to say consciousness or awareness has humans and animals, and not the other way around.

THE FINAL
FREEDOM AND THE
NEW WORLD

If you have made it this far in this book, you have likely recognized, to some extent, the Still Point as your true, unchanging nature. This recognition of the simple aware-being that you are is the beginning, and ultimately the culmination, of the great upward movement of humanity to discover its purpose in the universe. It is the answer to all of the great philosophical, spiritual, and true scientific questions of mankind. It is the true arrival of understanding—the understanding of the complete unity of life and all life-forms that have been or could ever be. It is the great sigh of relief heaved when one has awoken from a bad or confusing dream only to recognize that they are the dreamer who is forever safe from the threats and fears of the dream world. Because this realization is transpersonal, it excludes no one as there is no one who stands apart from this unlimited ocean of self-aware being. The Still Point is the self-aware being that allows every sentient creature to know their experience. It is the life force of anything deemed living. It is unbroken and imperishable and utterly untouched by the loss of the body or the mind. The concepts of death, or lack, are laughable in the face of its unborn and uncreated reality.

Mankind has loitered in the garden of self-imposed separation and isolation for far too long. The baseless belief in being separate, individual beings has brought wars, strife, and planetary destruction unbefitting our true heritage. We have overlooked our true nature and placed our identities in the continually changing and unstable forms of our thoughts, feelings, and bodily identification. And we wonder why we are a fearful, anxious people, hell-bent on protecting and defending our self-created and ultimately nonexistent "islands of self." We accumulate bad advice in the form of toxic conditioning from the continual stream of "inputs" we have accepted from news or media outlets when most are feverishly driving the egoic agenda of fear and separation. We gladly accept the recommendation of a profoundly sick society to look for advice and inspiration from the famous or wealthy, not because they have found peace and happiness, but because they conform to society's misplaced ideal of materialistic success. We continue to search for lasting happiness by identifying ourselves with ever-increasing subdivisions of gender, sexuality, race, and nationality, while our true nature is utterly oblivious to such artificial distinctions and equally open and accepting of them all.

All the time we toil on the battlefield of conflicting thoughts, emotions, and perceptions of the everyday world, failing to recognize that one short step above that battlefield lies the untouchable peace of our ever-aware nature. From this lofty perch, we can engage in the world without being bound to any of its outcomes. Just as invincible as a player in a virtual reality video game, we can play our role from this place of inclusion and love. When we truly see "others" and even the seemingly solid world as one, in essence, we stop resisting what is and peace and happiness become our new baseline. From this new perspective, we see the tragedies and injustices of the world as the natural outcome of ego-based confusion in the minds of those who have yet to recognize their nature as the Still Point. For those who have recognized their true self, there is no longer confusion and thus no longer a choice to be made between fear and love, isolation or union. We see all creatures as one in essence with us and act according to this new realization.

We are in the midst of the most comprehensive wave of awakening this planet has seen since humanity long ago traded its divine unity for the isolation of believing we were separate egoic selves. The recent global strife has had the unintended silver lining of bringing countless humans to realize the only way "out" of the insanity of this world is to ultimately venture within—within to the unwavering ocean of self-aware being that has never been at the mercy of the world and its events, despite the insistence of the egoic mind. Far from being hopeless or random, the strife of current world events has solidified in many the revelation that while we can never control the outward circumstances of life, we are always in sole control of how we interpret them. This is the only power we have ever had, and the only power we have ever needed. This simple power of discrimination allows us to withdraw our self-identity from the circumstances of the world, and the thoughts and feelings of the mind, to the Still Point that is their source, and our very being. With this simple yet profound shift, the peace and joy of your being remain unaffected by outside circumstances, no matter how tempestuous. This shift in you is also the very beacon of hope for those still wavering through the fields of fear. Without necessarily uttering a word or taking any action, your very presence will suggest a new possibility of peace that simply can't be found by the old means of seeking and resisting experience. And if it is your destiny to act or speak of this peaceful unity you have remembered, you will do so with the humility of inviting those who have yet to see their true nature back to the peace of themselves—the inheritance they have simply overlooked.

As people of this planet return, in ever-increasing numbers, to living as and from the Still Point (their true eternal nature), it is inevitable that the "outer" circumstances of the world will begin to reflect this in ever-increasing ways. The ego thought system, which has held man in its merciless grip for millennia, has never been capable of delivering the one thing that every human being seeks: happiness. Happiness is the sole inheritance of the minds who have looked within to discover their own source and substance. While it is inevitable that many will continue their belief in being separate, limited entities for some time, the solid ego-based structures of our civilization that have nurtured and supported this false foundation are beginning to crumble as more and more recognize their inherent futility. Regardless of the pace of change externally, this has always been, and will always be, a revolution of one. We can each only recognize the truth of ourselves, but because this recognition is not personal, it liberates all.

The recognition of the Still Point as the shared being of all sentient creatures is love itself. It is the cure for the brutal wound of separation that has plagued humanity and brought this planet to the edge of destruction. Once this is clearly seen, there will no longer be any questions as to how to treat other humans, animals, or the planet itself. As even a very small percentage of humanity shifts to the understanding of our shared unity, the potential for a golden age on this earth will emerge. The destruction and neglect of centuries of humanity's ignorance can be reversed in a relatively short time. New epochs of art, science, medicine, and technology informed by this truth will be given the best chance to flourish. Yet all of these macro-level changes can only occur with the individual recognition that individuality itself was a painful illusion. Because it was but an illusion, it only needs to be seen as such for the clear truth of our ever-present, self-aware being to emerge from the thick veil of thoughts and emotions that have seemed to obscure it. In reality the Still Point, our aware-being, shines in the midst of all experience and must simply be given attention to emerge as our very freedom from the self-imposed prisons of false identity created by our minds. The simple felt sense of being that we experience when we ask ourselves, "Am I aware?" is the gateway to understanding. It is by continually returning to this recognition that it becomes obvious, over time, that *we are that* very awareness. This awareness that we are the Still Point becomes our very teacher. It is only in the immense silence of its teaching that we can break free of the bonds of time and space, and the fear those bonds encapsulate. No one is excluded from this truth. This truth is the final freedom that can only be denied by the mind that refuses to look deep inside itself for the peace it continually seeks.

The perennial wisdom at the heart of all major religious and spiritual systems has directed us to "go within" to the source of our mind, to find the lasting peace and happiness that resides there, and only there. Throughout the ages in all cultures and traditions, there have been those who have discovered this and gained their freedom. The time has come for this realization to become the new, normal state of humanity's understanding. From here, we can return to the playful dance of paradise this earth was made to be. Personally, and collectively, leaving behind the strife and confusion that the belief in separation fostered, we can all walk together onto the new lawns of Eden, for they were always waiting deep within us for our glorious return.

ABOUT THE
AUTHOR

Kevin Krenitsky has been, at times, a professional rock musician, a medical doctor and a business executive. Despite leading a life deemed outwardly "successful," he lived with a deep background of anxiety, fear, and stress that waxed and waned since early childhood. At the age of forty, in the midst of decades of suppressing tremendous inner and outer conflict, he reasoned there must be another way. This "willingness" led to a decade of studying non-duality by way of *A Course in Miracles*. Later, at the height of a successful business career, he turned away into relative isolation and soon found the direct path to the recognition of our true nature. One day in meditation, a thought came that a book called *The Still Point* would be written. Five years later the first words arrived.